Foundations of Modern Sociology Series

Alex Inkeles, *Editor*

The Sociology of Ideology, *Daniel Bell*
Science and Society, *Joseph Ben-David*
Deviance and Control, *Albert K. Cohen*
Modern Organizations, *Amitai Etzioni*
The Family, *William J. Goode*
Society and Population, *David M. Heer*
What Is Sociology? An Introduction to the Discipline and Profession, *Alex Inkeles*
Theory and Method in the Social Sciences, *Paul F. Lazarsfeld*
Person and Society: An Introduction to Social Psychology,
        Daniel J. Levinson and Alex Inkeles
The Sociology of Small Groups, *Theodore M. Mills*
Social Change, *Wilbert E. Moore*
The Sociology of Religion, *Thomas F. O'Dea*
Societies: Evolutionary and Comparative Perspectives, *Talcott Parsons*
The System of Modern Societies, *Talcott Parsons*
Changing Rural Societies, *Irwin T. Sanders*
The American School: A Sociological Analysis, *Patricia C. Sexton*
The Sociology of Economic Life, *Neil J. Smelser*
Social Stratification: The Forms and Functions of Inequality, *Melvin M. Tumin*

Foundations of Modern Sociology Series

the system
of modern societies

Talcott Parsons, *Harvard University*

Prentice-Hall, Inc., *Englewood Cliffs, New Jersey*

Prentice-Hall Foundations of Modern Sociology Series

Alex Inkeles, *Editor*

Current printing (last digit):
10 9 8 7 6 5 4 3

PRENTICE-HALL INTERNATIONAL, INC., London
PRENTICE-HALL OF AUSTRALIA, PTY., LTD., Sydney
PRENTICE-HALL OF CANADA, LTD., Toronto
PRENTICE-HALL OF INDIA PRIVATE LIMITED, New Delhi
PRENTICE-HALL OF JAPAN, INC., Tokyo

13–881540–2 (p)   13–881557–7 (c)

preface

This volume is conceived as a companion to my earlier contribution to the *Foundations of Modern Sociology* series, *Societies*: Evolutionary and Comparative Perspectives. Indeed, the two were originally conceived as a single volume but it proved impossible to bring even a very succinct discussion of the relevant material within the space limits of the series.

The time interval between the two publications has been regrettably long, with most of the responsibility falling on the author, both through the pressure of other commitments which he had assumed and through difficulties in organizing the material of the manuscript. Indeed I was rescued in part from these difficulties by the publisher's decision to extend the space limits somewhat, so that while the text of *Societies* extends only to 117 pages, the present volume runs to 143.

At first sight it may appear that, since it deals with a far shorter time period and narrower comparative range than did *Societies*, the task of composing a short book on the present topic would be considerably easier. I did not find this to be true. The sheer complexities of the relatively near landscape are far more obvious that those of far distant hills and mountains, but, perhaps as a phase of this magnification of the near (in time), there is a kind of involvement in subtle combinations of diagnostic and evaluative judgement which multiplies the difficulties of clear and objective statement. The difficulty of the short book in this situation of course lies in the impossibility for an author of anything like full exposition not only of the primary facts, but of his own judgments and their grounding in explanatory analysis. These disadvantages are of course balanced by the advantage of the pressure to be both accurate and clear within the limits of a very concise statement.

In the Preface as well as the very brief Introduction, I must emphasize the importance to me of the title of the book, namely the "System of Modern *Societies*," with special stress on the use of the last word in the plural. Among social science writings, this is an unusual emphasis, asserting as it does, first that not all social systems, even transnational ones, are "societies"; and second that the plural modern societies are not necessarily random variants but may in important senses constitute a system, the units of which are both differentiated from each other and are interdependently integrated with each other. This interdependence of course emphatically includes the factors of tension and conflict which are so conspicuous.

My indebtedness to others is even more salient for this volume than for its predecessor. Victor Lidz again performed entirely indispensable services, as the canvasser and winnower of relevant literature, and as general sounding board and critic in many discussions of substantive problems. When it came to the "crunch" of getting the manuscript within tolerable limits of length, including of course stylistic editing, the brunt function could not have been competently performed without intensive mutual communication on the substantive problems to the clarification of which Mr. John Akula contributed immensely. Finally, I am again grateful for the understanding support of the Editor of the Series, Alex Inkeles, to the publishers, and to my secretary in the decisive period, Miss Sally Nash.

Talcott Parsons
December 1970

preface

contents

introduction, 1

one

theoretical orientations, 4

two

Action Systems and Social Systems. The Concept
of Society. The Subsystems of Society. Modes
of Integration in Increasingly Differentiated Societies.
Processes of Evolutionary Change.

pre-modern foundations
of modern societies, 29

three

Early Christianity. The Institutional Heritage of
Rome. Medieval Society. The Differentiation of the
European System. Renaissance and Reformation.

vii

**the first crystallization
of the modern system, 50**

four

The Northwest. Conclusion.

**counterpoint and
further development:
the age of revolutions, 71**

five

*The Differentiation of Europe in the Age of
Revolutions. The Industrial Revolution. The
Democratic Revolution.*

**the new lead society
and contemporary modernity, 86**

six

*The Structure of the Societal Community. The
Educational Revolution and the Contemporary Phase
of Modernization. Pattern Maintenance and
Societal Community. Polity and Societal Community.
Economy and Societal Community. Conclusion.*

new counterpoints, 122

seven

*The Soviet Union. The "New Europe."
Modernization of Non-Western Societies.*

**conclusion:
the main pattern, 138**

eight

selected references, 144
index, 147

introduction

one

The thesis underlying this volume, and defining
its relation to *Societies*,[1] is that the modern type of society has emerged
in a single evolutionary arena, the West, which is essentially the area of
Europe that fell heir to the western half of the Roman Empire north of
the Mediterranean. The society of Western Christendom, then, provided
the base from which what we shall call the "system" of modern societies
"took off." Whether or not there is justification for treating medieval
Western Christendom as a single society, the succeeding territorial states—
and the cultural heritages that we call national—developed to such an
extent that, for the modern period, the whole complex can be viewed
only as a *system of societies.*

This book has many intellectual roots. Perhaps the most influential
is German idealism, as it passed from Hegel through Marx to Weber.
Although it is fashionable today to ridicule Hegel's glorification of the
Prussian state, he did develop a sophisticated theory of general societal
evolution and its culmination in the modern West; but like Marx's theory,
it had too definite a temporal closure. Marx recognized that feudalism

[1] Talcott Parsons, *Societies: Evolutionary and Comparative Perspectives* (Englewood Cliffs, N.J.: Prentice-Hall, 1966).

1

was not confined to Europe, but felt that the emergence of capitalism had enabled Europe to take the lead in general societal development, so that the final phase of socialism—communism—*had* to originate there.

Weber provided a more subtle theoretical justification for distinguishing Western modernity from the highest evolutionary level attained by the other principal civilizations. Even those who questioned Weber's propositions about the role of religion in bringing about this high level of evolution must agree that long after the process of modernization had begun in the West, no comparable developments had occurred elsewhere. Indeed, we shall argue that the modern system has extended beyond Europe only by colonization or, as in Japan, by processes in which the model of the modern West has been indispensable. In the introduction to his comparative studies in the sociology of religion,[2] Weber raised the question of whether or not the modern West has universal significance. Citing science based on experiment, the fine arts, rational systems of law and administration, the modern state, and "rational bourgeois capitalism," he concluded that the *combination* of such factors constitutes a unique sociocultural system with unparalleled adaptive capacity.

The present book is written in the spirit of Weber's work but attempts to incorporate the developments in sociological theory and other fields of the past fifty years. One important difference in perspective has been dictated by the link between organic evolution and that of human society and culture. Developments in biological theory and in the social sciences [3] have created firm grounds for accepting the fundamental continuity of society and culture as part of a more general theory of the evolution of living systems.

One aspect of this continuity is the parallel betwen the emergence of man as a biological species and the emergence of modern societies. Biologists agree completely that there is only one human species and almost completely that this species had only one evolutionary origin. From this origin man emerged, differentiated from other species by his capacity to create, learn, and use symbolic systems (culture) in the forms of language and other media. In this sense all human societies are "cultural"; and if possession of culture is the relevant criterion of human *society*, collective organizations in other species are properly called *protosocieties*.

---

[2] This introduction provides a valuable perspective on Weber's work not only in the sociology of religion but also more generally. For this reason and despite the fact that it was written in 1919, more than fifteen years after *The Protestant Ethic*, a translation of it was included in Max Weber, *The Protestant Ethic and the Spirit of Capitalism*, trans. by Talcott Parsons (New York: Scribners, 1930).

[3] Our position is presented in *Societies* and in "Evolutionary Universals in Society" in Talcott Parsons, *Sociological Theory and Modern Society* (New York: Free Press, 1967), Chap. 15. See also G. G. Simpson, *The Meaning of Evolution* (New Haven: Yale University Press, 1949); and Ernst Mayr, *Animal Species and Evolution* (Cambridge, Mass: Harvard University Press, 1963).

2

introduction

It is reasonable to suppose that the evolutionary path from the earliest human societies to the present ones involved major jumps in adaptive capacity. Our thesis is that the emergence of the modern system of societies, through a complex process lasting several centuries, constituted such a jump.

Many will regard the associated theses that modern societies have greater generalized adaptive capacity than do all others and that they have a single Western origin as "culture-bound" and evaluative, but perhaps three qualifications will correct that impression. First, the adaptive capacity of a society is not necessarily the paramount object of human value. For many people certain aspects of personality, culture, organic well-being, or particular social patterns may be of greater value. Second, our assessment of the superior adaptive capacity of modern societies does not preclude the possibility that a "postmodern" phase of social development may someday emerge from a different social and cultural origin and with different characteristics. Third, because societies institutionalize culture, they are open to penetration from outside through contact with other cultures. Although closure of the genetic composition of *species* is enforced through cross-species sterility, discrete *cultures* can under certain conditions communicate fruitfully. Modern societies, for example, already include ingredients of diverse cultural origins, by no means all Western. As the process of cultural inclusion will probably go much farther than it has, the culminating version of the modern system may prove rather less parochial than many observers now expect or fear.

Deeper than these considerations, however, is the empirical and theoretical conviction that the salience of adaptive factors describes the "way human society is." Developments in sociological theory and growing evidence enables us to revise considerably the framework within which Weber interpreted "rational bourgeois capitalism." We shall not, however, challenge his broad orientation toward the development of Western civilization within the general pattern of human social evolution.

theoretical
orientations
two

Action Systems and Social Systems

We consider social systems [1] to be constituents of the more general system of action, the other primary constituents being cultural systems, personality systems, and behaviorial organisms; all four are abstractly defined relative to the concrete behavior of social interaction. We treat the three subsystems of actions other than the social system as constituents of its environment. This usage is somewhat unfamiliar, especially for the case of the personalities of individuals. It is justified fully elsewhere, but to understand what follows it is essential to keep in mind that neither social nor personality systems are here conceived as concrete entities.

The distinctions among the four subsystems of action are functional. We draw them in terms of the four primary functions which we impute to

---

[1] See Chapter 2 of *Societies: Evolutionary and Comparative Perspectives*, (Englewood Cliffs, N.J.: Prentice-Hall, 1966); and our articles "Social Systems and Subsystems" and "Interaction" in the *International Encyclopedia of the Social Sciences* (New York: Macmillan, 1968); and the introductory materials in T. Parsons, E. Shils, K. Naegele, and J. Pitts (eds.), *Theories of Society* (New York: Free Press, 1961).

all systems of action, namely pattern-maintenance, integration, goal-attainment, and adaptation.[2]

An action system's primary integrative problem is the coordination of its constituent units, in the first instance human individuals, though for certain purposes collectivities may be treated as actors. Hence, we attribute primacy of integrative function to the social system.

We attribute primacy of pattern-maintenance—and of creative pattern change—to the cultural system. Whereas social systems are organized with primary reference to the articulation of social relationships, cultural systems are organized around the characteristics of complexes of symbolic meaning—the codes in terms of which they are structured, the particular clusters of symbols they employ, and the conditions of their utilization, maintenance, and change as parts of action systems.

We attribute primacy of goal-attainment to the personality of the individual. The personality system is the primary *agency* of action processes, hence of the implementation of cultural principles and requirements. On the level of reward in the motivational sense, the optimization of gratification or satifaction to personalities is the primary goal of action.

The behavioral organism is conceived as the adaptive subsystem, the locus of the primary human facilities which underlie the other systems. It embodies a set of conditions to which action must adapt and it comprises the primary mechanism of interrelation with the physical environment, especially through the input and processing of information in the central nervous system and through motor activity in coping with exigencies of the physical environment. These relationships are presented systematically in Table 1.

There are two systems of reality which are environmental to action in general and not constituents of action in our analytical sense. The first is the *physical environment*, including not only phenomena as understandable in terms of physics and chemistry, but also the world of living organisms so far as they are not integrated into action systems. The second, which we conceive to be independent of the physical environment as well as of action systems as such, we will call "ultimate reality," in a sense derived from traditions of philosophy. It concerns what Weber [3] called "problem of meaning" for human action and is mediated into action primarily by the cultural system's structuring of meaningful orientations that include, but are not exhausted by, cognitive "answers." [4]

In analyzing the interrelations among the four subsystems of action—

2 The four-function theory is presented in our introductory essay, "An Outline of the Social System," in *Theories of Society*, pp. 30–79, and more briefly in *Societies*, p. 28.

3 Max Weber, *The Sociology of Religion* (Boston: Beacon Press, 1963).

4 Cf. Clifford Geertz, "Religion as a Cultural System" in Michael Banton (ed.), *Anthropological Approaches to the Study of Religion* (New York: Praeger, 1966).

Table 1   Action

Subsystems	Primary Functions
Social	Integration
Cultural	Pattern Maintenance
Personality	Goal Attainment
Behavioral Organism	Adaptation

* The shaded area represents the social subsystem's environment.

This table presents the barest schematic outline of the primary subsystems and their functional references for the *General System of Action,* of which the social system is one of four primary subsystems, that concentrated about integrative function. A somewhat more elaborate schema is presented in Table 1, p. 26 of *Societies;* and a general rationale of this schema has been presented in Parsons, "Some Problems of General Theory in Sociology" in John C. McKinney and Edward Tyriakian (eds.), *Theoretical Sociology* (New York: Appleton-Century-Crofts, 1970).

and between these systems and the environments of action—it is essential to keep in mind the phenomenon of *interpenetration.* Perhaps the best-known case of interpenetration is the *internalization* of social objects and cultural norms into the personality of the individual. Learned content of experience, organized and stored in the memory apparatus of the organism, is another example, as is the *institutionalization* of normative components of cultural systems as constitutive structures of social systems. We hold that the boundary between any pair of action systems involves a "zone" of structured components or patterns which must be treated theoretically as *common* to *both* systems, not simply allocated to one system or the other. For example, it is untenable to say that norms of conduct derived from social experience, which both Freud (in the concept of the Superego) and Durkheim (in the concept of collective representations) treated as parts of the personality of the individual, must be *either* that *or* part of the social system.[5]

It is by virtue of the zones of interpenetration that procsses of interchange among systems can take place. This is especially true at the levels of symbolic meaning and generalized motivation. In order to "communicate" symbolically, individuals must have culturally organized common codes, such as those of language, which are also integrated into systems of their social interaction. In order to make information stored in the central nervous system utilizable for the personality, the behavioral or-

[5] Talcott Parsons, "The Superego and the Theory of Social Systems" in *Social Structure and Personality* (New York: Free Press, 1964).

6

theoretical orientations

ganism must have mobilization and retrieval mechanisms which, through interpenetration, subserve motives organized at the personality level.

Thus, we conceived social systems to be "open," engaged in continual interchange of inputs and outputs with their environments. Moreover, we conceive them to be internally differentiated into various orders of subcomponents which are also continually involved in processes of interchange.

Social systems are those constituted by states and processes of social interaction among acting units. If the properties of interaction were derivable from properties of the acting units, social systems would be epiphenomenal, as much "individualistic" social theory has contended. Our position is sharply in disagreement: it derives particularly from Durkheim's statement that society—and other social systems—is a "reality *sui generis.*"

The structure of social systems may be analyzed in terms of four types of independently variable components: values, norms, collectivities, and roles.[6] Values take primacy in the pattern-maintenance functioning of social systems, for they are conceptions of desirable types of social systems that regulate the making of commitments by social units. Norms, which function primarily to integrate social systems, are specific to particular social functions and types of social situations. They include not only value components specified to appropriate levels in the structure of a social system, but also specific modes of orientation for acting under the functional and situational conditions of particular collectivities and roles. Collectivities are the type of structural component that have goal-attainment primacy. Putting aside the many instances of highly fluid group systems, such as crowds, we speak of a collectivity only where two specific criteria are fulfilled. First, there must be definite statuses of membership so that a useful distinction between members and nonmembers can generally be drawn, a criterion fulfilled by cases that vary from nuclear families to political communities. Second, there must be some differentiation among members in relation to their statuses and functions within the collectivity, so that some categories of members are expected to do certain things which are not expected of other members. A role, the type of structural component that has primacy in the adaptive function, we conceive of as defining a class of individuals who, through reciprocal expectations, are involved in a particular collectivity. Hence, roles comprise the primary zones of interpenetration between the social system and the personality of the individual. A role is never idiosyncratic to a particular individual, however. A father is specific to his children in his fatherhood,

[6] See Talcott Parsons, "General Theory in Sociology" in R. K. Merton, L. Broom, and L. S. Cottrell, Jr. (eds.), *Sociology Today* (New York: Basic Books, 1959, and Harper, 1965).

7

but he is a father in terms of the role-structure of his society. At the same time, he also participates in various other contexts of interaction, filling, for example, an occupational role.

The reality *sui generis* of social systems may involve the independent variability of each of these types of structural components relative to the others. A generalized value-pattern does not legitimize the same norms, collectivities, or roles under all conditions, for example. Similarly, many norms regulate the action of indefinite numbers of collectivities and roles, but only specific sectors of their action. Hence a collectivity generally functions under the control of a large number of particular norms. It always involves a plurality of roles, although almost any major category of role is performed in a plurality of particular collectivities. Nevertheless, social systems are comprised of *combinations* of these structural components. To be institutionalized in a stable fashion, collectivities and roles must be "governed" by specific values and norms, whereas values and norms are themselves institutionalized only insofar as they are "implemented" by particular collectivities and roles.

The Concept of Society

We define society as the type of social system characterized by the highest level of self-sufficiency relative to its environments, including other social systems.[7] Total self-sufficiency, however, would be incompatible with the status of society as a subsystem of action. Any society depends for its continuation as a system on the inputs it receives through interchanges with its environing systems. Self-sufficiency in relation to environments, then, means stability of interchange relationships and capacity to control interchanges in the interest of societal functioning. Such control may vary from capacity to forestall or "cope with" disturbances to capacity to shape environmental relations favorably.

The physical environment has an adaptive significance for a society in that it is the direct source of the physical resources which the society can exploit through its technological and economic mechanisms of production. The allocation of access to physical resources, in order to be linked with the division of labor through the ecological aspect of society, requires a territorial distribution of residential locations and economic interests among the various subgroupings of the population. The physical environment has a second significance for societies in that, because of the importance of physical force as a preventive of undesired action, effective societal goal attainment requires control of actions within a territorial area. Hence, there are two contexts of societal self-sufficiency that con-

[7] See *Societies*, Chapter 2.

8

theoretical orientations

cern, respectively, economic and political functioning in relation to the physical environment, through technology and through the organized use of force in the military and police functions.

A third context of societal self-sufficiency concerns the personalities of individual members in a special mode of interpenetration with the organisms involved. The organism links directly to the territorial complex through the importance of the physical location of actions. But its main link with the social system involves the personality; this primary zone of interpenetration concerns the status of *membership*. A society can be self-sufficient only in so far as it is generally able to "count on" its members' performances to "contribute" adequately to societal functioning. No more than in the other interchanges involved in self-sufficiency, need this integration between personality and society be absolute. Yet one could not speak of a society as self-sufficient if the overwhelming majority of its members were radically "alienated."

The integration of members into a society involves the zone of interpenetration between the social and personality systems. The relation is basically tripartite, however, because parts of the cultural system as well as parts of the social structure are internalized in personalities, and because parts of the cultural system are institutionalized in the society.

At the social level, the institutionalized patterns of *value* are "collective representations" [8] that define the *desirable types* of social system. These representations are correlative with the conceptions of types of social systems by which individuals orient themselves in their capacities as members. It is the members' consensus on value orientation with respect to their own society, then, that defines the institutionalization of value patterns. Consensus in this respect is certainly a matter of degree. Hence self-sufficiency in this context concerns the degree to which the institutions of a society have been *legitimized* by the consensual value commitments of its members.[9]

At the cultural level, social values comprise only part of a wider system of value, since all other classes of objects in the action system must be evaluated too. Values are related to such other components of a cultural system as empirical knowledge, expressive symbol systems, and the constitutive symbolic structures that compose the core of religious systems.[10] Ultimately, values are mainly legitimized in religious terms.

---

[8] "Collective Representations" is a concept introduced by Durkheim to designate the cultural basis of social organization. He used it especially in his analysis of religion. We shall treat values, in Weber's sense, as special forms of collective representatives. See Talcott Parsons, *Structure of Social Action* (New York: Free Press, 1968), Chapter 11.

[9] Cf. "An Outline of the Social System," in *Theories of Society*.

[10] See Talcott Parsons, "Introduction" to the section "Culture and the Social System" in *Theories of Society*.

In the context of cultural legitimation, then, a society is self-sufficient to the extent that its institutions are legitimized by values that its members hold with relative consensus *and* that are in turn legitimized by their congruence with other components of the cultural system, especially its constitutive symbolism.

It is essential to remember that cultural systems do not correspond exactly with social systems, including societies. The more important cultural systems generally become institutionalized, in varying patterns, in a number of societies, though there are also subcultures within societies. For example, the cultural system centering on Western Christianity has, with certain qualifications and many variations, been common to the whole European system of modernized societies. Two modes of the relation of one society to other societies are discussed in the present book. First, all societies we speak of as "politically organized" are involved with various other societies in "international relations" of various types, friendly or hostile. We shall extend this conception and regard these relations as themselves constituting a social system which can be analyzed with the same general concepts as other types of social system. Second, a social system may be involved with the social structure and/or the members and/or the culture of two or more societies. Such social systems are numerous and of many different kinds. American immigrant families often retain effective kinship relations with people in the "old country," so that their kinship systems have both American and foreign "branches." Something similar can be said of many business firms, professional associations, and religious collectivities. Although the Roman Catholic Church, for example, is a social system, it clearly is not a society since its self-sufficiency is very low by our criteria. Its control of economic resources through the organization of production is minimal; it lacks autonomous political control of territorial areas; in many societies, its members constitute a minority. Thus we must take account of both social systems which are "supersocietal" in being comprised of a plurality of societies and social systems that are "cross-societal" in that their members belong to a plurality of different societies.

The Subsystems of Society

In accord with our four-function scheme for analyzing systems of action, we treat a society as analytically divisible into four *primary* subsystems (as shown in Table 2). Thus, the pattern-maintenance subsystem is particularly concerned with the relations of the society to the cultural system and, through it, ultimate reality; the goal-attainment subsystem or the polity, to the personalities of individual members; the adaptive subsystem, or the economy, to the behavioral organism and, through it, the physical world. These divisions are clearest and most

theoretical orientations

Table 2   Society (more generally, social system)

Subsystems	Structural Components	Aspects of Developmental Process	Primary Function
Societal Community	Norms	Inclusion	Integration
Pattern Maintenance or Fiduciary	Values	Value Generalization	Pattern Maintenance
Polity	Collectivities	Differentiation	Goal Attainment
Economy	Roles	Adaptive Upgrading	Adaptation

This table attempts to spell out, a little more elaborately, a four-function paradigm for the *society*, or other type of social system, conceived as an integrative subsystem of a general system of action. The societal community, which is the primary subsystem of reference for the present analysis, is placed in the left hand column; the other three follow it. Corresponding to this set is a classification in the second column, by the same functional criteria, of four main structural components of social systems. In the third column follows a corresponding classification of aspects of process of developmental change in social systems which will be used extensively in the analysis that follows. Finally, the fourth column repeats the designation of four primary functional categories.

Except for the developmental paradigm, this schema was first fully presented in the author's "General Introduction, Part II: An Outline of the Social System" in *Theories of Society*. For general comparison with Tables 1 and 2, please consult *Societies*, Tables 1 and 2, pp. 28 and 29, and the accompanying explanatory note.

important for societies advanced on the scale of modernity. However, the complexity of the relationships, both among subsystems of action and among subsystems of society, prevent these divisions from ever being very neat. For example, kinship structures must be located in all three of the above-mentioned subsystems. Through their relation to food, sex, biological descent, and residence, they are involved with the organism and the physical environment. As the individual's primary source of early learning of values, norms, and modes of communication, they are very much involved with the pattern-maintenance system. As the primary source of socialized services, they are involved with the polity.

Within this framework, the core of a society as a social system is the fourth component, its integrative subsystem. Because we treat the social system as integrative for action systems generally, we must pay special attention to the ways in which it achieves—or fails to achieve—various kinds and levels of internal integration. We will call the integrative subsystem of a society the *societal community*.

Perhaps the most general function of a societal community is to articulate a *system* of norms with a collective organization that has unity and cohesiveness. Following Weber, we call the normative aspect the system of legitimate order; [11] the collective aspect is the societal community

[11] Max Weber, *The Theory of Social and Economic Organization* (New York: Oxford University Press, 1947).

as a single, bounded collectivity. Societal order requires clear and definite integration in the sense, on the one hand, of normative coherence and, on the other hand, of societal "harmony" and "coordination." Moreover, normatively-defined obligations must on the whole be accepted while conversely, collectivities must have normative sanctions in performing their functions and promoting their legitimate interests. Thus, normative order at the societal level contains a "solution" to the problem posed by Hobbes —of preventing human relations from degenerating into a "war of all against all."

It is important not to treat a structure of societal norms as a monolithic entity. Hence we distinguish four components analytically, even though they overlap greatly in specific content. Our distinctions concern the grounds of obligations and rights as well as the nature of sanctioning noncompliance and rewarding compliance or unusual levels of performance.

The Core: The Societal Community

Our core category, the societal community, is relatively unfamiliar—probably because it is generally discussed in religious and political rather than social terms. In our view the primary function of this integrative subsystem is to define the obligations of *loyalty* to the societal collectivity, both for the membership as a whole and for various categories of differentiated status and role within the society. Thus in most modern societies willingness to perform military service is a test of loyalty for men, but not for women. Loyalty is a readiness to respond to properly "justified" appeals in the name of the collective or "public" interest or need. The normative problem is the definition of occasions when such a response constitutes an obligation. In principle loyalty is required in any collectivity, but it has a special importance for the societal community. Organs of government are generally the agents of appeals to societal loyalty as well as agents of implementation of the associated norms. However, there are many instances in which government and justified community agency do not directly coincide.

Particularly important are the relations between subgroups' and individual's loyalties to the societal collectivity and to other collectivities of which they are members. *Role-pluralism*, the involvment of the same persons in several collectivities, is a fundamental feature of all human societies. On the whole, an increase in role-pluralism is a major feature of the differentiation processes leading toward modern types of society. Therefore, the regulation of the loyalties, to the community itself and to various other collectivities, is a major problem of integration for a societal community.

Individualistic social theory has persistently exaggerated the significance of individual "self-interest" in a psychological sense as an obstacle

theoretical orientations

to the integration of social systems. The self-interested motives of individuals are, on the whole, effectively channeled into the social system through a variety of memberships and loyalties to collectivities. The most immediate problem for most individuals is the adjustment of obligations among the competing loyalties in cases of conflict. For example, the normal adult male in modern societies is both an employee and a member of a family household. Although the demands of these two roles often conflict, most men have a heavy stake in fulfilling loyalties to *both*.

A societal community is a complex network of interpenetrating collectivities and collective loyalties, a system characterized by both functional differentiation and segmentation. Thus kinship-household units, business firms, churches, governmental units, educational collectivities, and the like are differentiated from each other. Moreover, there are a number of each type of collective unit—for example, a very large number of households, each comprised of only a few persons, and many local communities.

Loyalty to the societal community must occupy a high position in any stable hierarchy of loyalties and as such, is a primary focus of societal concern. However it does not occupy the highest place in the hierarchy. We have stressed the importance of cultural legitimation of a society's normative order because it occupies a superordinate position. It operates in the first instance through the institutionalization of a value-system, which is part of both the societal and the cultural systems. Then its sub-values, which are specifications of general value patterns, become parts of every concrete norm that is integrated into the legitimate order. The system of norms governing loyalties, then, must integrate the rights and obligations of various collectivities and their members not only with each other, but also with the bases of legitimation of the order as a whole.[12]

In its hierarchial aspect, the normative ordering of the societal community in terms of memberships comprises its *stratification* scale, the scale of the accepted—and, so far as values and norms are integrated, legitimized—*prestige* of subcollectivities, statuses, and roles and of persons as societal members. It must be coordinated both with universal norms governing the status of membership and with the elements of differentiation among the functions of subcollectivities, statuses, and roles, which do not as such imply a hierarchy. The concrete stratification system, then, is a complex function of all these components.

Role-pluralism renders the problem of the status of individuals in a stratification system especially complex. Stratification mechanisms have generally treated individuals as diffusely integrated in large collective systems, membership in which defines their status. Lineages, ethnic groups, "estates," and social classes have operated in this way. However

[12] On these matters, see Robert N. Bellah, "Epilogue," in *Religion and Progress in Modern Asia* (New York: Free Press, 1965).

13
theoretical orientations

modern society requires a differentiation of individual statuses from diffuse background solidarities, giving modern systems of stratification a distinctive character.[13]

The position of a subcollectivity or individual in the stratification system is measured by the level of its or his *prestige* or capacity to exercise *influence*. Influence we conceive to be a generalized symbolic medium of societal interchange, in the same general class as money and power. It consists of the capacity to bring about desired decisions on the part of other social units without directly offering them a valued *quid pro quo* as an inducement or threatening them with deleterious consequences. Influence must operate through persuasion, however, in that its object must be convinced that to decide as the influencer suggests is to act in the interest of a collective system with which both are solidary. Its primary appeal is to the collective interest, but generally on the assumption that the parties involved have particular interests in promoting the collective interest and their mutual solidarity. Typical uses of influence are persuasion to enter into a contractual relation "in good faith" or to vote for a specific political candidate. Influence may be exchanged for *ad hoc* benefits or for other forms of influence, in a sense parallel to that in which monetary resources may either be used to obtain goods or pooled or exchanged. Influence may also be exchanged for other generalized media such as money or power.[14]

Societal Community and Pattern-Maintenance

The bases of cultural legitimation transcend direct contingencies of influence, interests, and solidarity, being grounded at the societal level in *value commitments*. By contrast with loyalty to collectivities, the hallmark of a value-commitment is greater independence from considerations of cost, relative advantage or disadvantage, and social or environmental exigency in the meeting of obligations. The violation of a commitment is defined as illegitimate: its fulfillment is a matter of honor or conscience which may not be comprised without dishonor and/or guilt.

Although this may sound very restrictive, as indeed such commitments often are, the degree and kind of restrictiveness involved depends on a variety of factors. Commitment to values in general implies the assumption of an obligation to help implement them in concrete action. Especially where the value system is "activistic," as it generally is in modern societies, this implies realistic acceptance of certain conditions of collective action.

[13] Talcott Parsons, "Equality and Inequality in Modern Society, or Social Stratification Revisited," *Sociological Inquiry*, 40/2 (Spring 1970).
[14] Talcott Parsons, "On the Concept of Influence," *Politics and Social Structure* (New York: Free Press, 1969).

14

Thus, value *systems* contain a category of commitments to "valued association," solidarity in legitimate collective relationships and enterprises. What associations are valued is a matter that varies widely among societies. It is almost impossible to ensure the legitimacy of association by restricting legitimation to quite specifically defined acts, however, because actors need scope for considerable discretion if they are to implement their values under varying circumstances. One major factor in setting the breadth of this scope is the level of generality of the legitimating values. For example, an injunction not to exploit others in economic transactions is very different from a specific prohibition of lending money at interest. The *generalization* of value systems, so that they can effectively regulate social action without relying upon particularistic prohibitions, has been a central factor in the modernization process.

At the cultural level, the relevant aspect of values is what we ordinarily call moral. It concerns the evaluation of the objects of experience in the context of social relationships. A moral act implements a cultural value in a social situation involving interaction with other actors. As a matter of interaction, it must involve standards which bind the interactors reciprocally.

Moral values comprise only one component of the value-content of a cultural system, others being, for example, aesthetic, cognitive, or specifically religious values. Cultures also become differentiated on bases other than the moral, so that religion, art as expressive symbolization, empirical knowledge (eventually science), also become independent, differentiated cultural systems. A highly differentiated cultural system along with complex modes of articulation, is a hallmark of modern societies.[15]

Societal Community and the Polity

In addition to the aspects of a societal normative order centering about membership and loyalty and about cultural legitimation, we must consider a third. Influence and value-commitments operate voluntarily, through persuasion and appeal to honor or conscience. However, no large and complex social system can endure unless compliance with large parts of its normative order is *binding*, that is negative situational sanctions attach to noncompliance. Such sanctions both deter noncompliance—in part by "reminding" the good citizen of his obligations—and punish infraction if, as, and when it occurs. The socially organized and regulated exercise of negative sanctions, including threats of using them when intentions of noncompliance are suspected, we call the function of *enforcement*. The more highly differentiated a society, the more likely en-

[15] Talcott Parsons, "Introduction" to "Culture and the Social System" in *Theories of Society.*

theoretical orientations

forcement is to be performed by specialized agencies such as police forces and military establishments.[16]

Regulated enforcement requires some mode of determining the actual fact, agency, and circumstances of the infraction of norms. Among the specialized agencies that operate in this connection are courts of law and the legal profession. A complex normative order requires not only enforcement, however, but also authoritative interpretation. Court systems have very generally come to combine the determination of obligations, penalties, and the like for specific cases with interpretation of the meaning of norms, often a very general problem.[17] Less developed societies tend to reserve the latter function to religious agencies, but modern societies entrust it increasingly to secular courts.

These problems raise questions about the relation between a societal community and the polity. In our analytical terms, the concept *political* includes not only the primary functions of government, in its relation to a societal community, but also corresponding aspects of any collectivity.[18] We treat a phenomenon as political in so far as it involves the organization and mobilization of resources for the attainment of the goals of a particular collectivity. Thus business firms, universities, and churches have political aspects. In the development of modern societies, however, government has increasingly become differentiated from the societal community as a specialized organ of the society that is at the core of the polity.

As it has become differentiated, government has tended to center on two primary sets of functions. The first concerns responsibility for maintaining the integrity of the societal community against generalized threats, with special but not exclusive reference to its legitimate normative order. This includes the function of enforcement and a share in the function of interpretation, at least. Moreover, the general process of governmental differentiation creates spheres within which it becomes admissible explicitly to formulate and promulgate new norms, making legislation part of this function also. The second primary function, the executive, concerns collective action in whatever situations indicate that relatively specific measures should be undertaken in the "public" interest. This responsibility ranges from certain inherently essential matters, such as defense of territorial control and maintenance of public order, to almost any issue deemed to be "affected with a public interest."[19]

[16] Talcott Parsons, "Some Reflections on the Place of Force in Social Process" in *Sociological Theory and Modern Society* (New York: Free Press, 1967).

[17] Extremely suggestive in this regard is Lon Fuller, *The Morality of Law* (New Haven: Yale University Press, 1964).

[18] Talcott Parsons, "The Political Aspect of Social Structure and Process" in David Easton (ed.), *Varieties of Political Theory* (Englewood Cliffs, N.J.: Prentice-Hall, 1966). (Reprinted in *Politics and Social Structure.*)

[19] *Ibid;* see also Gabriel A. Almond and G. Bingham Powell, *Comparative Politics; A Developmental Approach* (Boston: Little, Brown, 1966).

16

theoretical orientations

The basic relations between government and the societal community may be ascribed. Even early modern societies defined the common people as simply "subjects" of a monarch, ascriptively obligated to obey his authority. Fully modern levels of differentiation, however, have tended to make the power of political leadership contingent on the support of very extensive proportions of the population. In so far as this is true, we shall distinguish roles of political leadership from positions of authority more generally.

Differentiation between leadership and authority necessitates special generalization of the medium we call power.[20] We define power as capacity to make—and "make stick"—decisions which are *binding* on the collectivity of reference and on its members in so far as their statuses carry obligations under the decisions. Power must be distinguished from influence for the promulgation of binding decisions differs importantly from attempts to persuade. By our definition, a citizen exercises power when he casts his vote because the aggregate of votes bindingly determines the electoral outcome. Only a little power still is power, just as one dollar, though only a little money, very definitely is money.

Societal Community and the Economy

A fourth component of the normative order concerns matters of practicality. Its most obvious fields of application are the economic and technological; its governing principle is the desirability of efficient management of resources. Even where issues of collective loyalty, binding obligations, and morality are not involved, the action of an individual or collectivity will be disapproved if it is unnecessarily wasteful or careless. In modern societies, the normative aspect of these considerations is especially clear in the regulation of the use of labor as a factor of production in the economic sense. Commitment to the labor force involves an obligation to work effectively within the legitimate conditions of employment.[21] As Weber noted, there is a crucial moral element in this obligation. But short of the moral emphasis, rational economic and technological action is very generally approved, while deviation from the relevant standards of rationality is disapproved.

The differentiation of autonomous structures necessitates the development of a generalized monetary medium in association with a market system. Money and markets operate where there is a sufficiently complex division of labor and where spheres of action are sufficiently differentiated from political, communal, or moral imperatives.[22] Of the generalized

[20] Talcott Parsons, "On the Concept of Political Power," in *Politics and Social Structure.*

[21] Neil J. Smelser, *The Sociology of Economic Life* (Englewood Cliffs, N.J.: Prentice-Hall, 1963).

[22] *Ibid*; see also Talcott Parsons and Neil J. Smelser, *Economy and Society* (New York: Free Press, 1956).

mechanisms of societal interchange, money and markets is the least directly involved with the normative order as it centers in the societal community. Hence, practical rationality is regulated mainly by institutional norms, above all the institutions of property and contract which have other bases of sanction.[23]

Methods of Integration in
Increasingly Differentiated Societies

The Legal System

What we have been treating as the societal normative order comes very close to what is generally meant by the concept of law. Much discussion of the law stresses the criteria of bindingness and enforceability, associating law primarily with government and the state. Other lines of analysis stress the consensual elements in the normative validity of law, a theme which permits emphasis on the importance of its moral legitimation. We treat law as the general normative code regulating action of, and defining the situation for, the member units of a society.[24] It is comprised of the components just reviewed integrated into a single system.

Very generally, modern legal systems contain constitutional components, whether written as in the United States or unwritten as in Britain. In the zone of interpenetration between the pattern-maintenance system and the societal community, the constitutional element defines the main outline of the normative framework governing societal relationships in general—as in the American Bill of Rights. On modern levels of differentiation, such content is clearly not religious, since its normative validity is framed for the societal system, not the full range of action in general. Indeed, there has been a modern tendency to dissociate specific religious commitment from the constitutional rights and obligations of citizenship. Because religious affiliation generally involves the formation of collectivities, it must always be articulated in the societal community. However, the two need not be coextensive.

Neither is the constitutional element "purely moral," for moral considerations too extend over a wider range than do societal values. Constitutional norms articulate with the societal community and involve the component of societal loyalty in the form of valued association; law concerns the morality of citizenship, but not necessarily all morality. Further-

---

[23] The classic analysis of the significance of property and contract for social systems was developed by Emile Durkheim in *The Division of Labor in Society* (New York: Macmillan, 1933).

[24] Cf. Fuller, *op. cit.*; also his *Anatomy of the Law* (New York: Praeger, 1968).

theoretical orientations

more, the moral element can provide the grounds for legitimized revolts against a societal normative order, varying from minor civil disobedience to revolution.

Although the constitutional element is presumptively enforceable, enforcement always raises a question of whether the organs of government are legitimately acting in a constitutional—and back of that a moral—sense. Hence, a second aspect of the constitutional element is the normative definition of the broad functions of government, including the extent and limitations on powers of the various governmental agencies. Constitutional law in this sense becomes increasingly important as the societal community comes to be differentiated from its government. The powers of government then need specific justification, for the societal community would not be adequately protected from arbitrary uses of power if it were to grant blanket legitimacy to its "rulers" to act upon their own interpretations of the public interest.[25]

It is crucial that "executive" authority comes to be differentiated from the governmental functions that have direct constitutional relevance. In pre-modern societies explicit legislation as a differentiated function is minimal, because the normative order is mainly *given* in a tradition or founding revelation. Hence, the legitimation of a continuing legislative function is a distinctively modern development. With a good many qualifying complications, it has tended to require that the legislative process should actively involve the societal community through a system of representation. The trend has been to make the power to legislate contingent upon the legislators' interaction with the interested elements of the community, ultimately the total electorate in most modern societies.[26] Indeed, a similar contingency generally applies to occupants of executive authority. The changeability of the law, which has resulted from these developments, has made it particularly important to have differentiated provision for concern with the "constitutionality" of law. Although the American system of judicial review is special in various respects, modern constitutions have very generally established some agency that is not purely governmental, especially in the executive sense, to pass judgment on constitutional issues.

It is under this broad constitutional framework that the lower order functioning of the legal system proceeds. It consists in the making of binding decisions, for the most part by officially "authorized" agencies (usually courts of law), and in various processes of their implementation by administrative procedures. It is particularly important that the extraconstitutional content of law is not confined to specific acts of legislation, nor

[25] On our usage of the concept of legitimation, compare Weber, *The Theory of Social and Economic Organization.*

[26] Cf. Parsons, "The Political Aspect of Social Structure and Process" in *Varities of Political Theory.*

to publicly binding decisions of executive agencies. It also includes elements of both the legal tradition generated in court decisions that stand as precedents, and the "administrative law" of generalized "rulings," rather than particular case decisions, promulgated by administrative agencies (but subject to legislative and judicial review).

Our whole discussion of normative order and its relation to the polity applies in principle to *any* social system, although the relation between government and the societal community is of principal importance. One source of this importance is that in general, only government is authorized to use socially organized physical force as an instrument of compulsion. Indeed an effective governmental monopoly of force is a major criterion of integration in a highly differentiated society.[27] Moreover, only government is entitled to act for the societal collectivity as a whole in contexts of collective goal-attainment. Any other agency that directly presumes to do so commits a revolutionary act *ipso facto*.

Membership in the Societal Community

In discussing the legitimate order of society, we have frequently referred to the collective aspect of the societal community. Our multiple criteria of a society indicate that the relation between these two primary aspects must be complex, especially in that the jurisdiction of the norms cannot neatly coincide with community membership. The most obvious discrepancy derives from the territorial basis of societies. Territorial jurisdiction requires that normative control is to some extent independent of actual membership in the societal community. For example, temporary visitors and long term "resident aliens," as well as the property holdings of "foreign" interests, must be regulated.

These considerations indicate that a particularly important part of the relation between the normative and the collective aspects of a societal community concerns their mutual relations to government. Government cannot simply "rule," but must be legitimized in governing a relatively bounded community by taking responsibility for the maintenance of its normative order. At one extreme, the principal content of the normative order may be considered more or less universal to all men. However, this raises acute problems of how far such highly universalistic norms can be effectively institutionalized in the actual operations of so extensive a community. At the other extreme, both government and the normative order may apply only to a particular small community. Within the broad range of variation between these extremes, modern societal communities have generally taken a form based upon nationalism. The development of this form has involved both a process of differentiation between societal com-

[27] Weber, *The Theory of Social and Economic Organization.*

theoretical orientations

munity and government and reform in the nature of societal community, especially with respect to membership.

The immediate background for the development was, for the most part, a more or less "absolute" monarchy in which the individual was considered a "subject" of his king. It was important that this "direct" relation of subject to sovereign replaced the tangle of particularistic solidarities which characterized feudal society. However, the "subject" pattern of societal membership was in turn replaced by a citizenship pattern.

The first phase in the development of the citizenship complex was the creation of a legal or civic framework that fundamentally redefined the boundary-relations between the societal community and the government or "state."[28] A critical aspect of the new boundaries was the definition of "rights" of the citizen, the protection of which became an important obligation of government. In the early phase, the protection of rights probably went farthest in English Common Law of the 17th century. However, it was a pan-European development that also produced the German conception of the *Rechtsstaat*. The process was simplified in Protestant areas because the citizens had to deal with only one main focus, the political authority, which organizationally controlled the church as well as the state.[29] In England the first phases of religious toleration within Protestantism comprised an essential part of the broader process of establishing citizen rights.

The second main phase in the development of citizenship concerned participation in public affairs. Although the legal rights of the first phase did protect attempts to influence government, especially through rights of assembly and freedom of the press, the next phase institutionalized positive rights to participate in the selection of governmental leadership through the franchise. The spread of the franchise "downward" in the class structure has often been gradual, yet there has been a conspicuous common trend toward universal adult suffrage, the principle of one citizen, one vote, and secrecy of the ballot.[30]

A third main component of citizenship is "social" concern with the "welfare" of citizens, treated as a public responsibility.[31] Whereas legal rights and the franchise support capacities to act autonomously in the status of citizenship, the social component concerns the provision of realistic opportunities to make good use of such rights. Hence, it attempts

[28] Our entire discussion of citizenship is heavily in debt to T. H. Marshall's *Class, Citizenship, and Social Development* (Garden City, N.Y.: Anchor Books, 1965).
[29] Cf. Seymour Martin Lipset and Stein Rokkan, "Introduction" to *Party Systems and Voter Alignment* (New York: Free Press, 1968).
[30] Stein Rokkan, "Mass Suffrage, Secret Voting, and Political Participation" in *European Journal of Sociology*, II (1961): 132–52.
[31] Marshall, *op. cit.*

to ensure that adequate minimum standards of "living," health care, and education are available to the masses of the population. It is particularly notable that the spread of education to ever wider circles of the population, as well as an upgrading of the levels of education, has been closely connected with the development of the citizenship complex.

The development of modern institutions of citizenship has made possible broad changes in the pattern of nationality as a basis of the solidarity of the societal community. In early modern society, the strongest foundation of solidarity was found where the three factors of religion, ethnicity, and territoriality coincided with nationality. In fully modern societies however, there can be diversity on each basis, religious, ethnic, and territorial, because the common status of citizenship provides a sufficient foundation for national solidarity.

The institutions of citizenship and nationality can nevertheless render the societal community vulnerable if the bases of pluralism are exacerbated into sharply structured cleavages. Since the typical modern community unifies a large population over a large territory, for example, its solidarity may be severely strained by regional cleavages. This is particularly true where the regional cleavages coincide with ethnic and/or religious divisions. Many modern societies have disintegrated before varying combinations of these bases of cleavage.

Societal Community, Market Systems, and Bureaucratic Organization

Where societal solidarity is emancipated from the more primordial bases of religion, ethnicity, and territoriality, it tends to foster other types of internal differentiation and pluralization. The most important of these are based on economic, political, and associational (or integrative) functions. The economic category refers above all to the development of markets and the monetary instruments essential to these functions, which, we have noted, presuppose the institutionalization in new forms of contract and property relations. Thus, they rest on the "rights" component of citizenship, for an economy that is purely "administered" by agencies of central government would violate the freedoms of private groups to engage in market transactions autonomously. Once the market system of an economy is highly developed, however, it becomes very important to government as a channel for the mobilization of resources.

In the earlier phases of modernization, markets are primarily commercial, involving trade in physical commodities, and secondarily financial, involving operations of lending and borrowing. The large scale entrance of the primary factors of production into the market system is the principal hallmark of the "industrial" phase of economic development. In addition to the advances in technology, this centers on the social *organization* of

22

theoretical orientations

the productive process, involving new forms of the utilization of manpower in bureaucratic contexts.[32]

In discussing the political aspect of societies above, we were rather selective. We dealt primarily with the relation of government to the total societal community, stressing the direct articulation between them in the "support" system. This system concerns primarily the interaction of leadership elements, both within and aspiring to governmental positions, and elements of the social structure that are not directly involved in the governmental system as such. The processes of interaction comprise both the interchange of political support and leadership initiative, and the interchange of governmental decisions and "demands" from various interest groups. These interchanges constitute a system requiring a certain equilibration if the polity is to be stably integrated with the societal community.

The other principal operative structure of government is the administrative organization, including military establishment, through which policy decisions are implemented. In general, bureaucratization developed primarily though not exclusively, in governments. Among its most important features is the institutionalization of roles as *offices* that have relatively well defined spheres of official function, authority, and "power" that are separated from the incumbent's private affairs. Offices are differentiated on two bases, function performed for the organization and position in the hierarchy or "line" authority.[33]

The development of bureaucratic organization in general necessitates that the relevant form of office be an *occupational* role, an incumbent being "appointed" through some kind of "contract of employment." Hence his family's subsistence generally depends on his salary or wage remuneration. In turn, this requires a "labor market" for the allocation of human services in terms of negotiations over employment opportunities and conditions.

A major feature of an industrial economy is the bureaucratic organization of production and, correspondingly, the mobilization of manpower through labor markets. By a complex progression through a number of phases, the economy has produced an immense proliferation of bureaucratic organizations outside the governmental sphere. One principal stage was based upon the "family firm" of early industrial "capitalism," which was bureaucratized at the "labor" but not the managerial level.

We consider bureaucratic organization to be primarily political because it is oriented in the first instance to collective goal-attainment. In the case of the business firm the collectivity is a private group within the societal community; in the case of government it is the whole community

[32] Smelser, *op. cit.*

[33] Talcott Parsons, *Structures and Process in Modern Societies* (New York: Free Press, 1960), Chapters 1–5.

23

organized for collective goal-attainment. Nevertheless we treat employment as a form of membership in a collectivity, leaving aside the problem of its relations to membership through other modes of participation in economic enterprise. Of course, private bureaucracy is not confined to economic production, but is found in churches, universities, and many other types of collectivity.

The market systems we have discussed are involved in interchange between the economy and the pattern-maintenance system, on the one hand, and the economy and the polity on the other. They do not directly involve the societal community since its functions vis-à-vis these subsystems are regulative through the general normative order more than directly constitutive. We must also emphasize the distinction between the "commercial" markets, dealing with physical commodities, and the "labor" markets, dealing with human services, including those at high levels of competence and responsibility. From a sociological point of view, we find confusing the economists' common practice of treating "goods and services" together as *the* primary output of the economy.

Associational Organization

A third main type of structuring that modern societal collectivities make possible is the "associational." Perhaps the prototype of an association is the societal collectivity itself, considered as a corporate body of citizens holding primarily consensual relations to its normative order and to the authority of its leadership. A major trend of modern associations has been toward a certain egalitarianism, manifested most clearly and importantly in the three aspects of citizenship which we have discussed.

A second trend of associational structure is toward voluntariness. Of course, this principle can never be applied strictly to compliance with a normative order or collective decisions, for an element of bindingness is essential to all collectivities. However, it often applies almost literally to decisions to accept and retain membership, an alternative to compliance always being resignation. The relationship between the societal community and government, however, is special. Other associations exist under a general governmental and societal protection, but the very basis of security itself rests on the fundamental combination. Hence, elements of compulsion and coercion are present in the enforcement of the societal normative order that are absent in other cases. The equivalent of "resignation," which is emigration, entails a far heavier cost than does the relinquishment of other associational memberships. In principle it also entails accepting another societal-governmental order, whereas in the case of divorce, one need not remarry.

A third major characteristic of associational organization, which very

theoretical orientations

definitely applies to the societal collectivity and to governmental agencies, is the importance of procedural institutions.[34] Although particularly significant in the legal system, they also permeate the processes of associational decision-making, both at the level of representative bodies and at that of membership participation. In general, procedural systems consist of two levels, each governed by a code of rules. The first regulates the discussions by which interested parties may attempt to persuade the participants in the making of binding decisions. It has many forms, but generally meetings are conducted according to rules of order which a presiding officer is responsible for implementing. Discussion within associations is a primary sphere of the operation of influence as a medium for facilitating social process. From the viewpoint of an interested party, discussion serves to improve the chances of having his view prevail; from the viewpoint of the collectivity, it facilitates an approach to consensus.

The second level concerns the actual process of deciding itself. In courts of law, the deciding agency is a jury, judge, or panel of judges. However, by far the most common practice—within juries and judicial panels as elsewhere—is voting, with its general tendencies toward the principles of one member: one vote and the equal weighting of votes, the logical consequence of which is majority rule. In any case, decision by voting must follow rules fixed in advance, including the expectation that decisions arrived at by correct observance of the procedural rules will be accepted by all defeated elements. In such cases as the election of governmental leadership this may be a focus of very severe strain; implementing this requirement is a paramount test of the institutionalization of "democratic" solidarity.

Concurrent with the development of associationalism in government, there has been a vast proliferation of associations in other sectors of society. Political parties articulate with governmental process, but also with many sorts of associated "interest groups," most of which represent a variety of operative collectivities. There are also associations organized about innumerable "causes," as well as interests of diverse sorts, for example, recreational, artistic, etc.

In two broad contexts, highly important operative functions of modern societies are performed almost entirely by associational structures. The first is the involvement of "fiduciary" boards in the larger-scale sectors of business enterprise and in many other types of "corporate" organizations. In relation to "executive management," they somewhat parallel the relation of the legislature to the executive organs of a modern government. Sometimes the members of such boards are in some sense elected, e.g. by stockholders, but often not. In any case, they have largely replaced the

[34] Compare with Weber's concept of formal rationality in *Max Weber on Law and Society*, Max Rheinstein (ed.), (Cambridge: Harvard University Press, 1954).

kinship element as the "nonbureaucratic" top of the predominantly bureaucratic structures of business.[35] In the "private nonprofit" sector, too, ultimate control, especially in regard to financial responsibility, tends in some sense to be held by fiduciary boards.

The second very large associational development concerns the professions.[36] Though much professional function has traditionally been performed in the framework of individual "private practice," professionals have long tended to associate in order to advance their common interests, including the maintenance of professional standards of competence and integrity. Higher education has gained increasing prominence in this complex, not least in the training of practicing professionals. Hence, the profession of higher education, and of scholarly research, has also been acquiring greater relative importance. It is notable that the core structure of the academic profession, the faculty, is basically associational.

All three of the main types of operative organization (markets, bureaucracy and associational structures) have been growing increasingly prominent in the processes of differentiation and pluralization of modern societal communities.

Processes of Evolutionary Change

Although it has been the most prominent in the foregoing discussion, we consider differentiation to be one of *four* main processes of structural change which, interacting together, constitute "progressive" evolution to higher system levels. We call the other three processes adaptive upgrading, inclusion, and value generalization (in application to social systems).[37]

Differentiation is the division of a unit or structure in a social system into two or more units or structures that differ in their characteristics and functional significance for the system. We have already discussed a complex instance of differentiation: The emergence of both the modern family household and the modern employing organization from the more diffusely functioning peasant family household, which involved changes in many roles, collectivities, and norms. A process of differentiation results in a more evolved social system, however, only if each newly differentiated component has greater adaptive capacity than the component that previously performed its primary function.

[35] In *The Theory of Social and Economic Organization* Weber emphasizes that all bureaucracies must be headed nonbureaucratically.

[36] Talcott Parsons, "Professions" in the *International Encyclopedia of the Social Sciences.*

[37] This paradigm was originally presented in Talcott Parsons, "Some Considerations on the Theory of Social Change" in *Rural Sociology*, 26 (Sept. 1961): 219–39. It is also discussed in somewhat more detail with some revisions in *Societies*, Chapter 2.

26

theoretical orientations

Adaptive upgrading is the process by which a wider range of resources is made available to social units, so that their functioning can be freed from some of the restrictions on its predecessors. Modern factories require much more generalized commitments to render service from those who engage in production than did peasant households, but can produce a greater variety of goods much more economically.

The enhanced complexity of a system undergoing differentiation and upgrading necessarily raises problems of integration. In general, these problems can be met only by the *inclusion* of the new units, structures, and mechanisms within the normative framework of the societal community. For example, when employing organizations become differentiated from the family household, the authority systems of both types of collectivity must gain articulation within the society's structure of norms.

Finally, the foregoing processes must be complemented by *value generalization* if the various units in the society are to gain appropriate legitimation and modes of orientation for their new patterns of action. We noted above that the general value patterns of a society must be specified to the great variety of situations in which action is socially structured. We are now stating an obverse point, namely that when the network of socially structured situations becomes more complex, the value pattern itself must be couched at a higher level of generality in order to ensure social stability.

We also wish to call attention to one further aspect of processes of evolutionary development. In discussing the generalized media of interchange among units of a social system, namely influence, political power, money, and value commitments, we have attended primarily to their most obvious function of facilitating routine interchange among the differentiated units of social system. However, they may also facilitate creative increases in the extent and level of operations within social systems. Modern economists have shown that money, through the process of lending and investment, can be a primary instrument for increasing the level of economic production as well as for facilitating exchange in a system of division of labor. We have argued elsewhere that this fundamental property of money, i.e., its capacity for expanding economic productivity through the credit mechanism, has analogues in the operations of the other generalized media, above all power and influence.[38] Thus, the power mechanism can operate to increase the long-run effectiveness of the polity and influence can be used to enhance the capacity for solidarity of the societal community.

Briefly, anchorage in a higher-order subsystem of action is the basic condition of the upgrading effects of a generalized medium of interchange.

[38] Cf. T. Parsons, "On the Concept of Political Power" and "On the Concept of Influence," in *Politics and Social Structure*.

theoretical orientations

On a very broad basis, therefore, cultural development is essential for the evolutionary advance of social systems. For example, religious developments underlie all major processes of value generalization, and the advancement of empirical knowledge underlies the institutionalization of new technologies. Sufficient levels of value generalization, implemented above all through the legal system, are prerequisite to major steps of inclusion in the structure of a societal community. A consensual base that promotes adequately extensive operation of the influence mechanism is necessary for major developments in the system of political power. Certain degrees of heightened political integration are prerequisite to the expansion of money economies beyond relatively simple levels.[39]

39 See S. N. Eisenstadt (ed.), *Max Weber on Charisma* (Chicago: University of Chicago Press, 1968), esp. his "Introduction."

theoretical orientations

pre-modern
foundations of
modern societies
three

In *Societies* we discussed the development of cultural innovation in the small "seed bed" societies of ancient Israel and Greece. Our analysis focused upon the conditions under which major cultural advances could develop and eventually become dissociated from their societal origins. These two models were chosen because of their central contributions to later social evolution. Elements derived from "classical" Hebrew and Greek sources, after undergoing further basic development and combination, comprised some of the main cultural components of modern society. Their focus was Christianity. As a cultural system Christianity proved in the long run able both to absorb major components of the secular culture of antiquity and to form a matrix from which a new order of secular culture could be differentiated.

Christian culture—including its secular components—was able to maintain clearer and more consistent differentiation from the social systems with which it was interdependent than either of its forebears had been. Because of such differentiation from society, Christian culture came to serve as a more effective innovative force in the development of the total sociocultural system than had any other cultural complex that had yet evolved.

29

A cultural system does not, however, institutionalize itself; it must be integrated with a social environment that can fulfill the functional requirements for a currently viable society (or set of societies). Evolution involves continuing *interaction* between the cultural and social systems, as well as among their respective components and subsystems. The social prerequisites of cultural effectiveness thus not only change but also may at any given stage depend upon *previous* stages of the institutionalization of cultural elements.

In this perspective, the Roman Empire takes on a dual significance for our analysis. First, it constituted the principal social environment in which Christianity developed. As Roman society owed an immense debt to Greek civilization, Greek influence entered the modern system not only "culturally," through Christian theology and the secular culture of the Renaissance, but also through the structure of Roman society, especially in the East where the educated classes remained Hellenized after the conquest by Rome. Second, the heritage of Roman institutions was incorporated into the foundations of the modern world. It is crucial that Greek influence and the Roman institutional heritage were significant mainly for the *same* structures: The legal order of the Empire constituted an indispensable condition of Christian proselytization, thus engendering a congruence of pattern that was reflected in the inclusion of elements of Roman law in both the canon law of the Church and the secular law of medieval society and its successors.

We shall begin this analysis with sketches of the two primary social "bridges" between the ancient and modern world: Christianity and certain institutions of the Roman Empire. Then we shall skip a number of centuries in order to treat the more immediate background of modern society: feudal society and its culmination in the high Middle Ages, then the Renaissance, and the Reformation.

Early Christianity

Christianity originated as a sectarian movement within Palestinian Judaism. It soon broke with this religio-ethnic community however; the decisive event was St. Paul's decision that a Gentile might become a Christian without joining the Jewish community and observing Jewish law.[1] The early Christian Church then evolved into an associational religious group independent of *any* ascriptive community, either ethnic or territorial. Its focus was specifically religious, the salvation of the individual soul; in this respect it became especially differentiated from any secular social organization. It was thus gradually spread through-

[1] A. D. Nock, *St. Paul* (New York: Harper, 1938).

pre-modern foundations of modern societies

out the Roman Empire through the proselytizing of the apostles and other missionaries. Its main early success was among the humbler urban population—craftsmen, small merchants, and the like—who were bound neither by the traditionalism of peasant groups nor by the upper classes' vested interests in the status quo.[2]

In terms of religious content, the crucial elements of continuity with Judaism were transcendental monotheism and the conception of a covenant with God. A sense of having been "chosen" by God for a special divine mission thus continued. In classical Judaism the people of Israel had enjoyed this status; in Christianity it adhered to the company of professing *individuals* who gained access to eternal life through their adoption of the faith.[3] Salvation was to be found in and through the Church, especially after the sacraments had been crystallized. The early Church was a voluntary association, however, quite antithetical to a "people" in sociological type. The individual could only be a Jew as a *total* social personality, one of the "people"; but one could be *both* a Christian *and* an Athenian or Roman on the level of societal participation, a member of both the Church and an ethnic-territorial community. This step was crucial in differentiating both role and collectivity structures.

This new definition of the basis for the religious collectivity and its relation to secular society had to be legitimated theologically. The new element was Christ, who was more than simply another prophet or the messiah in the Jewish tradition; such figures had always been purely human with no claim to divinity. Christ was *both* divine and human, the "only begotten son" of God the Father, but also a man of flesh and blood. In this dual aspect, his mission was to offer salvation to mankind.

The transcendence of God the Father was the essential source of the sharp differentiation between what were later called the "spiritual" and "temporal" spheres. The basis for their integration was the relation of souls to God, through and "in" Christ and His Church, which was defined theologically as the "mystical body of Christ" and partook of the divinity of Christ through the Holy Spirit.[4] Christ not only offered salvation to souls but also freed the religious community from previous territorial and ethnic ascriptions.

The relations among the three persons of the Trinity—and of each to man and the other aspects of creation—were highly complex. A stable theological ordering of these relations required intellectual resources not present in prophetic Judaism. It was here that late Greek culture

[2] Adolf Harnack, *The Mission and Expansion of Christianity* (New York: Harper, 1961).
[3] Rudolf Bultmann, *Primitive Christianity* (Cleveland: Meridian, 1956).
[4] A. D. Nock, *Early Gentile Christianity and Its Hellenistic Background* (New York: Harper, 1964).

31

furnished its crucial contribution. The Christian theologians of the third century (especially the Alexandrian fathers Origen and Clement) mobilized the sophisticated resources of neo-Platonic philosophy to handle these complex intellectual problems,[5] thus also establishing a precedent for drawing upon secular culture in a way that has been closed to various other religious movements, notably Islam.

The conception of the Christian Church as both divine and human was of theological origin. Its conception as a voluntary association, with strong overtones of egalitarianism and corporate independence relative to the social environment, owed much to the institutional models of antiquity. St. Augustine's use of the term "city," essentially in the sense of polis, was a striking symbol.[6] Certainly the Church was an association of religious "citizens" parallel to the polis, particularly in the local congregation. As the Empire could be regarded as a federation of city-states, it too provided a relevant model as the growing movement came to require structures of authority for stabilizing relations among its local congregations. A certain centralization seemed appropriate, and the gradual establishment of the Roman papacy was the solution. Although the Church became differentiated institutionally from all secular organizations, it also became structurally more congruent with the society of its environment.

An important aspect of the differentiation of the Christian Church from secular society was its sharpness and clarity: The early Christians lived "in" the secular world but were not "of" it. The larger society was pagan and appeared to Christians radically devalued as a world of sin unredeemed. The famous admonition "render unto Caesar the things that are Caesar's" should be understood as a recognition of Caesar's being a pagan monarch, the symbol of a pagan political and social order. As an "acceptance" of Roman authority, it was an expression of Christian passivity in relation to all worldly things. As Troeltsch has emphasized so strongly, early Christianity was not a movement of social reform or revolution. Acceptance of Caesar was by no means an expression of positive integration, for it was rooted in eschatological expectations of the immediacy of the Second Coming, the end of the world, and the Last Judgment.[7]

The whole Christian movement contained a basic duality in its orientation toward the secular world, again largely as a heritage of Judaism. On one hand, it asserted the primacy of "eternal life" over *all* worldly concerns. Beside proselytization, it thus emphasized devotional and ascetic

[5] Werner Jaeger, *Early Christianity and Greek Paideia* (Cambridge, Mass: Harvard University Press, 1961).

[6] Charles Norris Cochrane, *Christianity and Classical Culture* (New York: Oxford University Press, 1957).

[7] Ernst Troeltsch, *The Social Teachings of the Christian Churches*, Vol. I (New York: Harper, 1960).

pre-modern foundations of modern societies

means to salvation. On the other hand, Christ and His Church, like the people of Israel, had a divinely appointed mission *for* this world, which in effect meant for human society. Although the situation of the Church within imperial society necessarily subordinated this component, its evolutionary potential was very great.

Christian aloofness from secular concerns was severely strained as an increasing proportion of the population was converted, particularly among the higher, socially and politically more responsible classes.[8] This process culminated during the early fourth century in a new imperial religious policy, reflected in the Edict of Milan (which proclaimed the toleration of Christianity), the conversion of the Emperor Constantine, and the adoption of Christianity as the state religion.[9]

This culmination was simultaneously a great triumph and a source of tremendous strains within Christianity, for the Church was in danger of losing its independence and becoming an instrument of secular political authority. Significantly, it was in this period that monasticism was established.[10] The Pauline admonition to "remain in that station in which you are called" had long seemed insufficiently radical to a minority of Christians, who renounced the world totally to become anchorites. This dynamism was now harnessed to the establishment of organized communities devoted to the fully religious life in withdrawal from the world under vows of poverty, chastity, and obedience.[11]

Although it was a "seed bed" movement carrying potentials for *future* societal change, Christianity could not transform the Roman Empire because the necessary conditions for its institutionalization were absent. The monastic movement, then, established another kind of "seed bed" *within* Christianity, exerting a powerful and increasing evolutionary leverage on both the "secular" church and secular society.

The institutional structuring of the Christian mission for the world, in which monasticism played an important part everywhere, came to be fundamentally bound up in the broad process of differentiation between the eastern and western branches of the Church. Partly as a result of the weakening of secular authority in the West, including the abandonment of Rome as the imperial capital, the Church had a much greater opportunity to become independently "activist" there. In organizing itself for the whole body of Christians, lay as well as clerical, the Western Church

---

[8] *Ibid.*

[9] Hans Lietzmann, *A History of the Early Church* (Cleveland: Meridian, 1961), esp. Vols. II and III.

[10] Paul Tufari, "Authority and Affection in the Ascetic's Status Group: St. Basil's Definition of Monasticism," unpublished doctoral dissertation, Harvard University.

[11] Herbert B. Workman, *The Evolution of the Monastic Ideal* (Boston: Beacon, 1962).

consolidated a "universal" episcopal system centralized under the see of Rome.[12] During the "Dark Ages" and much of the later medieval period, this organization was more effective than was any in the secular realm, through the long-run effects of three major developments.

First, a much more nearly legitimate place was established at the highest theological level for the "city of man," as distinguished from the "city of God," especially through the influence of Augustine. In contrast to the total alienation from secular society common under early Christianity, Augustinian thought "negatively tolerated" society, allowing its moral improvement through Christian influence as a legitimate endeavor.[13] Augustine also went considerably farther than his predecessors had done in accepting the secular culture of the ancient world.

Second, with the establishment of the Benedictine order, Western monasticism turned to a much greater concern with worldly matters than distinguished Eastern monasticism. This shift was accelerated with the establishment of other orders in the Western Church, for example the Cluniac monks, the Dominicans and Franciscans, and finally the Jesuits.

Third, the organization of the Church was cemented through the sacraments, which reached their final form before the Middle Ages. Priesthood was transformed into an *office*, independent of the personal quality of the incumbent and therefore of his particularistic connections.[14] The Western Church achieved a far higher level of "bureaucratic" independence for its secular priesthood than did the Eastern Church, whose bishops came to be drawn entirely from the monastic orders and whose parish priests were heavily involved in local communities.

The Institutional Heritage of Rome

The radical decline from the highest levels of civilization achieved by imperial Rome is well known, especially the disintegration of political authority in the West into a vast array of shifting tribal and regional groupings and authorities. This change was accompanied by virtual disappearance of a monetary and market economy and by reversion to local self-sufficiency and barter.[15]

When gradual revival and consolidation began, a significant new relation between church and secular authority emerged. The legitimation

---

[12] Lietzmann, *op. cit.*, esp. Vol. IV.
[13] Cochrane, *op. cit.*; and Troeltsch, *op. cit.*
[14] Max Weber, *The Sociology of Religion* (Boston: Beacon, 1963).
[15] H. St. L. B. Moss, *The Birth of the Middle Ages* (London: Oxford University Press, 1935); and Ferdinand Lot, *The End of the Ancient World and the Beginnings of the Middle Ages* (New York: Harper, 1961).

34

pre-modern foundations of modern societies

of Charlemagne's regime revolved around its relation to the church, as symbolized by his coronation by Pope Leo III in A.D. 800. This ceremony provided the model for the later Holy Roman Empire, which, though never a highly integrated polity, served as a legitimating framework for a unified Christian secular society.[16]

Within this institutional framework, the great medieval "synthesis" was characterized by *differentiation* between church and state—in the special medieval sense of the latter term. This differentiation came to be defined as that between the spiritual and the temporal "arms" of the Christian mission. The special mode of differentiation and integration formed the core of what Troeltsch considered the first version of the conception of a Christian Society.[17] The main institutional elements of Roman origin that survived through the Middle Ages were thus intimately bound up with the development of the Church.

The universalistic structures of Roman law had been gravely undermined during the migrations period by the principle of the "personality" of law, the judgment of a man according to the law of his own particular tribe.[18] This particularistic reference to tribal allegiance could only be overcome in jurisdiction and enforcement by the gradual revival of a *territorial* principle, for this aspect of law was intimately connected with the status of territorial political authorities. Although it was assumed that the secular law of the newly defined Empire was Roman law, the Empire was too loosely organized to constitute an effective agent of the detailed definition and enforcement of law. The legal tradition therefore tended to exert a kind of "cultural pressure," through its legitimating action, toward the establishment of territorial jurisdictions less extensive than was the Empire as a whole.[19]

Nevertheless, it was hardly even doubted that law in general meant Roman law and that the legal system of imperial Rome continued to be in force, even in English Common Law, which was less a new legal system than the adaptation of Roman law to English conditions.[20] Furthermore, the Church adopted much of Roman law for the regulation of its own affairs through the canon law and developed a class of legal experts within the clergy. Perhaps the "bureaucratization" of the medieval Church was less crucial than was its ordering in terms of a universalistic legal system.

[16] Henri Pirenne, A *History of Europe* (2 vols.; Garden City, N.Y.: Anchor, 1958).

[17] Troeltsch, *op. cit.*, Vol I.

[18] C. H. McIlwain, *The Growth of Political Thought in the West* (New York: Macmillan, 1932).

[19] *Ibid.*; and Otto von Gierke, *Political Theories of the Middle Ages* (Boston: Beacon, 1958).

[20] F. W. Maitland, *The Constitutional History of England* (Cambridge, Eng.: Cambridge University Press, 1908).

The firm territorial basis of political institutions is a second essential component of modern societies that owes more to the Roman heritage than to any other source. Despite the many differences between Roman and modern governmental institutions, the Roman heritage and model provided the crucial point of departure for the development of the early modern European state, not least through the legitimation inherent in assumed continuity of organization.[21]

A third major institutional heritage of the ancient world was the pattern of "municipal" organization. The Roman *municipium* had been derived from the city-state of earlier times: the Greek polis and the *urbs* of Rome and other Italian provinces. The *municipium* had long lost its political independence, yet it retained many of the old institutional patterns. Most important was the conception of its structural core as a corporate body of citizens. In certain basic respects the citizens of a *municipium* constituted a body of equals with shared legal and political rights and such obligations as military service. Although the *municipia* followed Rome itself in developing aristocracies of citizens with prestige and wealth, who monopolized public offices, their associational character was sufficiently preserved to contrast sharply with rural society, especially under feudalism. The survival of these communities constituted a major difference between pre-modern Europe and any Oriental society of comparable development.[22]

Medieval Society

The very considerable period of uneven development and transition between the end of the Middle Ages and the first crystallization of modern society largely resulted from the subtle combination in medieval society of features favoring modernization and features, basically incompatible with modernity, that could become foci of resistance to modernization. As a "type," feudal society was most sharply antithetical to the more advanced types that preceded and succeeded it. It represented a drastic regression of almost all the components of Rome's advanced society toward more archaic forms. Yet, once the point of maximum regression had been reached, recovery and dynamic advance were rapid. A key to this development is that feudalism, the product of retrogression, received only secondary legitimation. Although feudal loyalties were certainly romanticized and indeed blessed by the Church, this recognition was provisional and limited. On the whole, these loyalties were rather easily superseded by alternative claims that could appear both

[21] J. B. Morrall, *Political Thought in Mediaeval Times* (New York: Harper, 1962).

[22] Max Weber, *The City* (New York: Free Press, 1958).

pre-modern foundations of modern societies

older and newer and that were more deeply grounded in the culture, certain key components of which remained rather highly rationalized.

From the eleventh century on, elements that could engender primary legitimation began to assert themselves, initiating the process of differentiation and related developments that eventually produced the modern structural type. The general *direction* of this evolution was largely determined by advances within the "bridge" structures already discussed: the basic orientation of Western Christianity, the relative functional specificity of the Church's organizational structure, the territorial principle of political allegiance, the high status of the Roman legal system, and the associational structure of the urban community.

The fragmentation of imperial Roman social organization slowly gave way to the highly decentralized, localized, and structurally dedifferentiated type of society usually called "feudalism." [23] The general trend of feudalism was the elimination of a universalist base of order in favor of particularistic loyalties, originally "tribal" and local. Concomitantly the old elements of relatively egalitarian associational individualism tended to give way, at least at the level of fundamental political and legal rights, to diffuse hierarchical relations based on the inequality of the reciprocal duties of vassalage, protection, and service.

The feudal hierarchical relationship began as "contractual," in that the vassal agreed, through his pledge of fealty, to serve his lord in exchange for protection and other advantages.[24] In effect, it quickly became hereditary, however, so that, only when a vassal lacked a legitimate heir, could his lord freely select a "new man" to succeed him in a fief. For the peasants the feudal system established hereditary unfreedom through the institution of serfdom. One criterion of aristocracy was, however, full recognition of the legitimate heredity of status.

Provision for sheer physical security was probably the most pressing practical problem of the time. Beside the original "barbarian" invasion of the Empire, disorder throve on long-continuing incursions (for example, by the Muslims on the east and south, Huns on the east and north, and Scandinavians on the north and west) and constant internecine strife induced by political fragmentation.[25] A premium was thus placed on the military function, the basis of protection being military safeguards against violence. With strong support from the traditions of antiquity, a predominantly military class became ascendant in secular society and secured its position through the hierarchical institution of vassalage.

---

[23] For authoritative discussion relevant to sociological analysis, Marc Bloch *Feudal Society* (Chicago: University of Chicago Press, 1961) is by far the most useful single source on feudalism.

[24] F. L. Ganshoff, *Feudalism* (New York: Harper, 1961).

[25] *Ibid.*, Part I.

pre-modern foundations of modern societies

It became progressively less possible to maintain clear and simple feudal hierarchies, however. Relations became so ramified that many people held feudal rights and obligations within several potentially conflicting hierarchies. Although the liege relationship, which assumed primacy over all other obligations, was an attempt to solve this problem, it was more significant as a sign that the institution of kingship had not been completely feudalized but was reasserting its paramount prerogatives.[26]

After the eleventh century the territorial organization of the state, closely bound to the principle of kingship, gained steadily, if unevenly, in importance. Europe's gradually increasing population density, economic organization, physical security, and so on generally shifted the previously tenuous balance from feudal bases of organizational allegiance toward territorial bases. Concomitantly, there was an important crystallization of the institution of aristocracy, which can be viewed as a "compromise" between the territorial and feudal principles of organization.[27] In anything like its full flower, aristocracy was a late medieval phenomenon. It represented, at the macrosocial level, the focus of the two-class system from which the modern type of national secular social stratification developed.

Closely interdependent with the political feudalization of the early Middle Ages was drastic economic retrogression. The societal resource base became increasingly agricultural, finding a relatively stable focus in the institution of the manor. The manor was a local, relatively self-sufficient agricultural unit worked by an hereditary labor force dependent, in legally "unfree" status, on a feudal lord, generally an individual but frequently an ecclesiastical corporation like a monastery or cathedral chapter. The functional diffuseness of the manor was exemplified in the lord's status, which combined the roles of landlord, political leader, military commander, judicial authority, and shaper of economic organization.[28] Such diffuseness was suitable to the manor as a strong security base in the midst of feudal disorder but prevented it from providing the local organization necessary for modernization. That organization was much more closely approached in the towns.

We have held that, broadly speaking, the social structure of the Church was the primary institutional bridge between ancient and modern Western society. In order to influence evolution effectively, however, the Church had to be articulated with secular structures at strategic points. Weber emphasized that the European urban community offered precisely such a strategic point.[29] In Church contexts, differences of social class

26 Bloch, *op. cit.*
27 *Ibid.*
28 *Ibid.*, Part V; and Henri Pirenne, *Economic and Social History of Mediaeval Europe* (New York: Harvest, 1937), Part III.
29 Weber, *The City.*

pre-modern foundations of modern societies

were, in a special sense, downgraded though not eliminated within urban communities. Above all, the mass was open to the whole urban community without basic distinctions.[30] The nature of the religious component in urban organization was demonstrated most tangibly perhaps by the cathedral, which was never simply a building; it was an institution that, as both the seat of a bishopric and the focus of the cathedral *chapter*—an important collegial element in the Church structure—articulated two levels of Church organization.[31] The very considerable participation of the guilds in financing and building cathedral chapters and churches indicates that religious organization was closely associated with the economic and political aspects of the rising towns.

The crucial secular associational phenomenon in the towns was the emergence of the urban version of aristocracy, the patriciates—town-dwelling upper groups constituted as corporate entities. The major significance of these groups was their basic principle of organization, which ran counter to feudal principles of hierarchy.[32] They were organized in guilds, merchant guilds being the most prominent and influential. But the guild, itself following the pattern of the polis and *municipium*, was basically an *association of equals*.[33] Although there were guilds at various levels of prestige and power within the same urban community and in relation to its political structures and although the town could be variously located within the inclusive political structures of feudal society, the urban communities still presented organizational patterns conflicting with feudalism but consonant with the main course of later development.[34]

Probably the most important evolutionary developments in the early medieval period occurred in the Church, the only structure that was sufficiently inclusive to affect basic institutional patterns throughout Europe. The papacy of Gregory VII in the late eleventh century was perhaps the turning point. The Church had already renewed its interest in the broad philosophical-theological issues involved in establishing a thoroughly Christian body of knowledge that could serve as a guide to realizing the Christian society.[35] The first of the great Scholastic

[30] In rural areas the common pattern was for the lord of the manor to attend mass in his chapel whereas the commoners in his service attended church in the village or at a nearby monastery or town, if at all. Any noble of consequence had a priest as his own chaplain. No doubt it is significant in this context that Thomas Aquinas held that the urban way of life favored Christian virtue more than the rural way of life could. See Troeltsch, *op. cit.*, Vol. II, p. 255.

[31] R. W. Southern, *The Making of the Middle Ages* (New Haven: Yale University Press, 1953), pp. 193–204.

[32] Bloch, *op. cit.*, p. 416.

[33] Henri Pirenne, *Early Democracies in the Low Countries* (New York: Harper, 1963).

[34] Henri Pirenne, *Mediaeval Cities* (Princeton: Princeton University Press, 1925), esp. Chapter II, "Municipal Institutions."

[35] Southern, *op. cit.* and Troeltsch, *op. cit.*

syntheses was in the offing. The revival of systematic studies in the canon law and the Roman secular law—which Gregory himself encouraged —had already begun. The critical development at the level of social structure, however, was probably Gregory's insistence on a monastic degree of religious discipline in the church as a whole combined with his general assertion of strong Church interests in secular society.[36] He and some of his successors pushed the power and structural independence of the Church to points that opponents believed asserted its hegemony over secular structures. Such hegemony would have been inconceivable in the Byzantine Empire.

In some respects Gregory's major innovation was his insistence that the *secular* clergy observe celibacy.[37] Just when hereditary elements, as distinct from the more "personal" element of fealty, were rapidly gaining importance in the feudal system, he radically removed the priesthood, especially the bishoprics, from the sphere of hereditary consolidation. Whatever the sexual morality of secular priests, they could not have legitimate heirs, and their priestly offices could not become specifically institutionalized functions of kinship status, as monarchy and aristocracy were becoming. This insulation could not be entirely destroyed even by the common practice of appointing the higher clergy from the nobility. Although priests, bishops, and, indeed, popes continued for many centuries to be chosen largely for their kinship affiliations, efforts to *legitimate* such choices on kinship grounds were generally repudiated, even though the hereditary principle was becoming entrenched in many secular contexts. The tension between the Church's spiritual universalism and feudalism's temporal particularism, which became manifest in both religious and secular organizational spheres, constituted a strong pressure against Western society's settling into a comfortable traditionalism.

The Differentiation of the European System

So far we have discussed medieval society in terms of component structures without reference to their differential arrangement in various geographical areas within the system. We shall now consider the extent to which the differentiation of Europe as a system was foreshadowed in the pre-modern stages by examining the varying distribution of the institutional components throughout Europe.[38]

[36] Morrall, *op. cit.*

[37] Henry C. Lea, *History of Sacerdotal Celibacy in the Christian Church* (New York: Macmillan, 1907).

[38] Bloch, *op. cit.*, presents a clear outline of these variations. His treatment first suggested that such a pattern can, with the appropriate modifications for developmental changes, be extended well past the first main stages in the development of the modern system, as this will be treated in the following chapters.

pre-modern foundations of modern societies

The social environment of the European system consisted of relations to other societies, which varied greatly with geographical location.[39] The social environment of the Northwest was not problematic, for it was protected by the Atlantic frontier, which at that time was not an arena of important societal and political interchange. In the south and east, however, the social environments were highly significant. Spain was partially occupied by the Moors for most of the medieval period, and relations with the Saracens in the eastern Mediterranean were crucial throughout the Middle Ages. To the southeast lay the Byzantine Empire, which at the end of this period fell to the Turks; Orthodox Christianity extended northward into what eventually became Russia. The eastern boundary was a zone of struggle and shifting balance on the two axes of religion and ethnic affiliation. The Poles, Bohemians, and Croats became primarily Roman Catholic, whereas the Russians and most of the southern Slavs became Orthodox. At the same time, from Austria northward there was an unstable border between the Germanic and Slavic peoples, a line that did not coincide with the religious boundary. A strategic enclave just east of the German area was the Hungarian ethnic group, a precipitate of the Hunnic invasions.

There was thus a broad east-west difference in the bounding environments of Europe, involving physical differences, the extent of previous penetration of Roman influence, and the consequences of the split between the Western and Eastern Churches. There were also broad north-south differences, based on the physical barriers of the Alps and the Pyrénées. Italy was the seat of government of the Roman Catholic Church but *never* of the Holy Roman Empire. Although Latin culture, grounded in language, penetrated Spain, France, and a few other border regions, the bulk of transalpine society was ethnically not Latin.

Italy played a special role in the constitution of medieval society for two principal reasons. First, it contained the seat of the Church and was the area where presumably the Church's influence was most highly concentrated. Second, Roman institutions were most firmly grounded there and were thus able to recover most rapidly after minimal feudalism.

Under medieval conditions the Church inevitably became politically and economically entwined with secular society to a point far beyond that in modern times. A particularly important aspect of this involvement was direct governmental jurisdiction of the popes in what became the Papal States. At the same time the general decentralization of medieval society permitted the urban component of the Roman heritage to become strongest in Italy. North of Rome Italy came to be organized predominantly

[39] See Oscar Halecki, *The Limits and Divisions of European History* (Notre Dame, Ind.: University of Notre Dame Press, 1962). Halecki gives a general survey of the evolution of geographical-social differentiation in Europe.

pre-modern foundations of modern societies

in city-state form. The upper classes of the northern urban communities developed into a sort of amalgam of rurally based, initially feudal aristocracies and urban "patriciates." They became a *town-based* upper class, however; even though its members owned most of the agricultural land, it was a very different class from the feudal aristocracy of the North.[40] These circumstances strongly inhibited the emergence, first, of a predominantly feudal structure and, later, of territorial states transcending the scale of political structure that could be controlled by a single central city. As the wider application of Roman law in secular society depended upon the development of territorial states, it did not flourish there until later. As had the city-states of antiquity, the Italian units eventually proved unable to maintain political integrity in a "great power" system. Nevertheless, Italy was perhaps the principal pattern-maintenance subsystem of European society at that stage, an essential seed bed for later developments, in secular as well as in ecclesiastical culture.[41]

The eastern frontier was generally the most highly feudal part of the European system, though it had a special pattern of its own, particularly in Germany, which was highly variegated.[42] Eastward from the Rhine Valley and northeast from the Baltic Sea, the urban component became progressively attenuated to the lowest level in Europe. Economic and cultural conditions were certainly more primitive than elsewhere, and the proximity of the frontier encouraged a greater military emphasis. The feudal structure and social stratification generally were more rigidly hierarchical than in the West, providing the basis for more authoritarian regimes. Hierarchical differentiation and political authority thus gained primacy over economic development and the extension of culture. In this connection, the resulting hierarchical political centralization was a special development of resources for political effectiveness that had important implications for the future of the system. The eastern frontier areas, then, played an adaptive role in the European system, developing organization to protect it from threats of a sociopolitical and, beyond that, cultural character.

The soil of major social and political innovation lay primarily in the Northwest. The significance of Paris as the center of the Scholastic philosophy and the university developments at Oxford and Cambridge certainly lay in cultural innovation. This geographical area also fostered a double social development of special importance, however. On the one hand, England and France became the early matrices of the territorial state—distinct from feudalism, though its development had feudal under-

<hr/>

[40] See F. Schevill, *The Medici* (New York: Harcourt, 1949).
[41] J. H. Plumb, *The Italian Renaissance* (New York: Harper, 1965), esp. Chapter 10.
[42] Bloch, *op. cit.*

42

pinnings.[43] On the other, there was a blossoming of urban communities centering mainly around the Rhine Valley, from Switzerland to the North Sea.

Both developments owed much to the organizational looseness of the Empire. Given the peripheral location of England and France, their kings were able from an early time to ignore allegiance to the Emperor. Many of the continental urban communities, on the other hand, became "free cities" of the Empire with substantial exemptions from the feudal structure and the developing territorial monarchies.[44] As these towns were generally also the seats of cathedrals, this position of strength was reinforced by alliance with the Church.

The processes that centered first in England and France constituted the earliest differentiation of the modern form of societal community. Developments in the free cities, very much in association with the Italian cities, initiated the further differentiation of the economy from political structures and from the societal community as such.

Neither of these forms of structural differentiation was compatible with a predominantly feudal organization. The early kings were both kings in the later sense and feudal magnates; theoretically they were the most important vassals of the Holy Roman Emperor, whereas their "barons" were in turn their feudal vassals in chief. As such, the feudal classes not only exercised governmental authority within their fiefs but also constituted the core of the societal community; they were ex officio, as it were, both the highest-prestige stratum and the symbolic focus of societal solidarity. The network of feudal solidarities that clustered about them constituted the main societal structure. The "lower classes" were bound into it through their unfree status on the manors; they were beholden directly only to their own lords. Virtually no civil administration reached down to the level of the lord of the manor, to say nothing of the serf. The main early exception was the king's prerogative of keeping the "peace," most firmly institutionalized in the English court system, through which he could intervene locally in major criminal matters and in quarrels between two feudal lords.[45] The multiplication of allegiances as feudalism developed encouraged further royal intervention and facilitated "national" integration.[46]

The feudal baronage gradually evolved into what became the aristocracies of early modern societies. Politically, perhaps the crucial development was the assumption by royal governments of the two closely related

[43] Charles Petit-Dutaillis, *The Feudal Monarchy in England and France* (London: Routledge, 1936).
[44] Even today Hamburg and Bremen are "free cities" within the West German Federal Republic.
[45] Maitland, *op. cit.*
[46] Bloch, *op. cit.*

prerogatives, first, of military command without feudal dependence upon contingents basically under the control of barons and, second, of direct taxation bypassing intermediate feudal echelons. The successors of the baronage, however, remained "socially" the class with the highest prestige, articulated with the monarchy, in that the king was always the "first gentleman" of the realm and the head of the aristocracy. With these developments, land holding tended to move away from the land*lord* status, which included political control of the people, as well as of the land, even though it remained the primary economic base of the aristocracy.

Where the forces promoting governmental organization over larger territories were weak, towns sometimes became fully independent. Beside creating a tradition of political independence that served as a strong brake on absolutism, the free-city zone also fostered most strongly the consolidation as an independent social stratum of the main alternative leadership group to the aristocracies, the bourgeoisie.[47] Its economic basis lay not in land ownership but in commerce and finance. Although craft guilds were prominent in the urban structure, the merchant guilds tended to be more important, especially in the leading towns.

On both sides of the Alps, towns came to be the main centers of the emerging market economy; their independence from the newly consolidated monarchies in England and France and from domination by the Empire was probably an essential condition. In the larger system the independent position of the Rhenish urban groups could not but strengthen the position of their confreres in England and France. Indeed, in certain circumstances, alliances between kings and the bourgeoisie, especially of the capital cities, constituted very important counters to the landed aristocracies, especially as postfeudal conditions emerged.

With the relative isolation and strong government that followed the Norman conquest, England achieved a higher degree of political centralization than existed on the Continent. At the same time, it turned away from royal absolutism, thanks to the solidarity of the new aristocracy recruited from the followers of William the Conqueror. Within a century and a half, the barons proved capable of sufficiently integrated corporate action to impose Magna Charta on their king.[48] This corporate solidarity was in turn related to the conditions that gave rise to Parliament. Under these conditions, the English aristocracy moved farther and faster from feudal anchorage than did any other, thus winning an especially significant position of power and influence in the emerging state.

England was long economically backward, compared to Flanders and some other areas of the Continent. The English political structure, how-

---

[47] Henri Pirenne, *Early Democracies in the Low Countries.*
[48] Maitland, *op. cit.*

pre-modern foundations of modern societies

ever, provided favorable soil for future economic developments, for the strength of the landed aristocracy vis-à-vis the crown placed the merchant classes in a position of *tertius gaudens*. In a very tentative way, then, England developed the ingredients for a future synthesis of movements toward differentiation.

Renaissance and Reformation

The Renaissance gave rise to a highly developed secular culture that was differentiated from the primarily religious matrix. Originating in Italy, it laid the foundations of the modern arts and intellectual disciplines, including notably the borderline category of legal culture. Indeed, theology itself was affected through feedback from the new elements of secular culture that later crystallized in philosophy.

The cultural components that went into the Renaissance extended not only back into the Middle Ages but even farther, into antiquity as well. Ancient culture itself, however, had not attained the same order of differentiation, for it always remained religious in a sense not true of Western culture after the Middle Ages. The most important single component of rationalized medieval culture, Scholastic philosophy, betraying its classical heritage especially in the Thomist use of Aristotle, was closely bound to the theological system and lacked the cultural autonomy of post-Renaissance thought.[49]

From the beginning the Church had incorporated and developed further very important elements of classical culture. What the Renaissance meant, then, was an enormous development of this heritage mainly on the secular side. In our analytical terms, it was a process of differentiation, but insofar as it made possible the reception of elements that had been "indigestible" by the less-differentiated previous cultural system, it was also a process of inclusion.

It is a crucial point that the development took place *within* the religious framework.[50] The Church and the aristocracies were thus the most important patrons of the new fine arts, the major part of which portrayed religious subjects for the embellishment of churches, monasteries, and other religious edifices. Artists, and later scientists, however, were increasingly drawn from laymen rather than clerics, and they went well beyond the builders and embellishers of the medieval cathedrals in developing corporate identities and autonomy as experts in their work.[51] The universities were not very conspicuously involved, except in a few

[49] Troeltsch, *op. cit.*, Vol. II; and McIlwain, *op. cit.*
[50] Troeltsch, *op. cit.*, Vol. II.
[51] See Joseph Ben-David, *The Sociology of Science* (Englewood Cliffs, N.J.: Prentice-Hall, 1971), for a discussion of Renaissance science.

areas, especially law. Nevertheless great strides were taken during this period in extending outside the Church the role of the more-or-less professional specialist in cultural matters. Although some of the later phases of the Renaissance penetrated into Protestant areas only after the Reformation, they too were not directly antireligious but were conceived and disseminated within the religious framework.

The Renaissance seems to have originated in the revival of the literary styles and interests of Latin antiquity, especially in the secular writings of the Humanists.[52] The revived themes rapidly had a major impact on the visual and plastic arts: architecture, painting, and sculpture. Only later did science attain a comparable level of sophistication, through processes of internal differentiation as well as more general differentiation of secular culture from the social matrix. For example, Leonardo was a master of both artistic and scientific elements, whereas Raphael was not a scientist or Galileo an artist. This differentiation was probably basic to many aspects of modern culture because the new science, which culminated well into the seventeenth century with Newton, formed the main point of reference for the first great wave of modern philosophy. This philosophy was in turn directly fundamental to the development of the complexes of secular knowledge that we call the "intellectual disciplines."

Renaissance art turned increasingly to secular subjects, often scenes taken from classical mythology (as in many of Botticelli's paintings), landscapes, portraits, and the like. But even when subjects were religious, certain new secular concerns may be discerned. Probably the primary symbolic focus of Italian Renaissance art was the Madonna and child. In strictly religious terms, this focus represented a significant shift away from the Crucifixion, the martyrdom of saints, and other such subjects. At the same time it emphasized, indeed glorified, the human family, particularly the mother-child relationship. Motherhood was made almost universally appealing by the portrayal of Mary as an attractive young woman who obviously loves her child. Does this symbolism not reflect the further shift of Christian orientation toward positive sanctioning of the right kind of secular order?

The Renaissance was not mainly a movement of synthesis; rather it was a period of rapid cultural innovation. Such great changes could hardly have occurred without some involvement of the highest levels of culture, however, namely both philosophical and theological. The dynamic character and diversity of Scholastic philosophy should alert us to this principle. Although Thomism became the central formulation for the late-medieval synthesis, there were numerous other movements also.

[52] Paul Oskar Kristeller, *Renaissance Thought: The Classic, Scholastic and Humanist Strains* (New York: Harper, 1961).

pre-modern foundations of modern societies

Perhaps most important was Nominalism, which, stimulated by both classical thought and themes drawn from Islamic philosophy, became the most advanced branch of Scholasticism. It was more directly open to empirical considerations and less inclined neatly to close the Christian world view than was Thomism.[53]

In a broad variety of other cultural spheres too the Renaissance was concerned not only with differentiating the religious and the secular but also with integrating them. Much as the Madonna symbol indicated greater concern with "things of this world," newer monastic movements, notably the Franciscan and Dominican orders, which were particularly interested in charity and intellectual matters, wielded greater influence. Renaissance humanistic and legal studies had fundamental philosophical and, indeed, theological overtones, many of which became particularly salient as the first great achievements of the new science gained attention and demanded consideration for their implications. In condemning Galileo, the Church certainly did not indicate simple indifference to his work. Not totally unrelated to the problems raised by Galileo was the earlier contribution of the great Florentine Machiavelli, the first European "social thinker" to be more interested in understanding how secular society actually worked than in justifying a specific religio-ethical point of view.

The Renaissance originated primarily in Italy and attained its highest development there. Very early, however, a similar movement, most visible in painting, began north of the Alps, also overlapping with medieval culture. Although it never developed as far in Germany as in Italy, it nevertheless produced eminent artists like Cranach, Dürer, and Holbein. It took hold early and attained very full development in Flanders and considerably later in Holland, where it continued into the Protestant era before culminating in the seventeenth century. Not only did this cultural development originate in a social setting comprised of city-states in Italy, but also its northern extension followed almost exactly the band of free urban communities centering in the Rhine Valley. No comparable development of the visual arts arose in the predominantly feudal areas that led in formation of the large territorial states.

The Reformation was an even more radical movement of cultural change and profoundly affected the relations between cultural systems and society. Its major cultural innovation was theological, the doctrine that salvation comes, in the Lutheran version, "by Faith alone," or, in the Calvinist predestinarian version, through the direct communion of the individual human soul with a sovereign God without *any* human intervention. This innovation deprived any Protestant church and its clergy of the "power of the keys," the capacity to mediate salvation through the

---

[53] McIlwain, *op. cit.*; and Kristeller, *op. cit.*

sacraments. Furthermore, the "visible" church, the concrete collectivity of human believers and their clerical leaders, was conceived of as a purely human association. The attribute of divinity, the status of the church as the "mystical Body of Christ," belonged only to the invisible church, the company of *souls* in Christ.[54]

On this basis human society could not consist, as Thomism had held, of two layers with profoundly different religious statuses: the Church, *both* divine and human, and purely human secular society. Rather, it was believed to consist of *one* society, *all* members of which were both "bodies" as secular beings and "souls" in their relations to God. This view represented much more radical institutionalization of the individualistic components of Christianity than had Roman Catholicism.[55] It also had profound egalitarian implications, which have taken long to develop, however—and have done so very unevenly.

A further consequence of the elimination of the priesthood's sacramental powers was that the special sphere that Roman Catholic tradition called "faith and morals," and in which the visible Church held guardianship over all persons, was gravely undermined. Although many Protestant movements have attempted to continue ecclesiastical enforcement in this sphere, there has been a strong inherent tendency in Protestantism to define it as ultimately the individual's own responsibility. Similarly, the crucial form of stratification *within* the medieval Church, the differentiation between laity and members of the religious orders, lost its legitimation in Protestantism. On the human level of a "way of life," all "callings" had the same basic religious status; the highest religious merit and perfection could be attained in secular callings.[56] This attitude included marriage—Luther himself left his monastery and married a former nun, symbolizing the change.

This major change in the relations between church and secular society has often been interpreted as a major loss of religious rigor in favor of worldly indulgence. This view seems a major misinterpretation, however, for the Reformation was much more a movement to upgrade secular society to the highest religious level. Every man was obligated to behave as a monk in his religious devotion, though not in his daily life; that is, he was to be guided mainly by religious considerations. It was a decisive turn in the process, which dated from early phases of Christianity, to permeate the "things of this world" with religious values and create a "City of Man" in the image of God.[57]

---

[54] *Ibid.*

[55] Max Weber, *The Protestant Ethic and the Spirit of Capitalism* (New York: Scribner, 1958).

[56] *Ibid.*

[57] *Ibid.*; Troeltsch, *op. cit.*, Vol. II; Ernst Troeltsch, *Protestantism and Progress* (Boston: Beacon, 1953); and Talcott Parsons, "Christianity" in *International Encyclopedia of the Social Sciences* (New York: Macmillan, 1968).

pre-modern foundations of modern societies

The institutionalization of this conception of a religiously grounded human society implied the possibility of establishing a societal community with a corporate character something like that of the Church itself, above all of the Protestant conception of a church that dispensed with the stratification in the Roman Catholic conception. For the larger types of secular society, this effort required a mode and level of political integration far surpassing those of the medieval and Renaissance period. The Reformation came to play a central part in legitimating some of the most important new territorial monarchies, most immediately the German principalities, with whom Luther formed alliances.[58] Not only were these alliances probably essential to the survival of the movement itself, but they also initiated a type of church-state organization that could develop further certain essential ingredients of modern society. In England the Reformation was percipitated somewhat differently when Henry VIII converted to Protestantism, opening the way for basic changes in the Church and in its relations with secular society.

Where Protestant *state churches* were formed, there was a tendency (except in England) toward both religious and political conservatism, especially in Lutherism, which prominently allied itself with territorial monarchical regimes. The Calvinist branch has been much more conspicuously involved in broad movements stressing the independence of religious groups from political authority,[59] most notably in the United States. Developments within American Protestantism made an early separation of church and state religiously, as well as politically, acceptable.

[58] G. R. Elton, *Reformation Europe* (Cleveland: Meridian, 1965).
[59] Important exceptions are discussed in J. J. Loubser, "Calvinism, Equality, and Inclusion," in S. N. Eisenstadt (ed.), *op. cit.*

the first
crystallization of
the modern system
four

We have chosen to date the beginning of the system of modern societies from certain seventeenth-century developments in the societal community, especially the bearing of religion on the legitimation of society, rather than, as is usual, from eighteenth-century evolution toward "democracy" and industrialization.

After the Reformation shattered the religious unity of Western Christendom, a relatively stable division arose, roughly along the north-south axis. All Europe south of the Alps remained Roman Catholic; a Roman Catholic "peninsula" thrust into northern Europe, with France as its most important component. Protestantism in Switzerland enjoyed the protection guaranteed by the special nature of Swiss independence. Although Vienna was predominantly Protestant at the start of the seventeenth century, the Hapsburgs were able to "recatholicize" Austria, aided by the Turkish occupation of Hungary, where Protestantism was strong.

As religious struggle intensified, the "southern tier" of political units consolidated. In the sixteenth century this consolidation involved a union of the two most important states, Austria and Spain, under the personal rule of the Hapsburg Emperor Charles V. The "middle" of this empire was protected by the Kingdom of Naples and Sicily, immediately adjacent to the Papal States. The presence of the papacy in Italy and the extent of Hapsburg power made continued effective independence of the Italian city-states impossible.

The Counter-Reformation enforced a particularly close alliance between Church and state, exemplified by the Spanish Inquisition. In comparison to the "liberal" trends within late medieval and Renaissance Roman Catholicism, the Counter-Reformation Church stressed rigid orthodoxy and authoritarianism in its organization. Civil alliance with the Church in enforcing religious conformity fostered the expansion and consolidation of centralized government authority. Such enforcement was undertaken in the name of the Holy Roman Empire, with its special religious legitimation and divinely ordained Emperor.[1] By that time the political structure of the Empire was far more integrated than it had been in the Middle Ages.

Nevertheless, the Empire was vulnerable, in that it centered in the loosely organized "German nation"—Austria's population was only partly German by that time, and the Hapsburgs had assumed the crowns of Hungary and Bohemia through personal unions. The Treaty of Westphalia, which had ended the bitter Thirty Years' War, had not only made Holland and Switzerland independent of the Empire, but had also drawn the religious line *through* the remaining parts; many of the German princes had chosen Protestantism for their domains under the formula *cuius regio, eius religio*. Far more than the defection from Rome of Henry VIII, this choice undermined the legitimation of the old secular structure of Christendom, for the Empire had been conceived as the "secular arm" of the Roman Catholic *system* of basic unity. The settlement was an uneasy compromise, acceptable only as an alternative to the indefinite continuation of a highly destructive war. Nevertheless, it ended any realistic expectation that a Roman Catholic European system could be restored.[2] For more than three centuries the heartland of the Counter-Reformation remained tenaciously resistant to many modernizing processes, citadels of monarchial legitimism, aristocracy, and semibureaucratic states of the older type.

Although the Protestants dreamed of prevailing throughout Western Christendom, they soon splintered into different branches and never developed a conception of unity corresponding to that of medieval Roman Catholicism.[3] This fragmentation furthered the development of independent territorial monarchies based on unstable integration of absolutist political regimes and "national churches."[4] It also, however, contained the seeds of the *internal* religious pluralism that was to advance rapidly in England and Holland.

[1] James Bryce, *The Holy Roman Empire* (rev. ed.; London: Macmillan, 1904).
[2] *Ibid.*
[3] Ernst Troeltsch, *The Social Teachings of the Christian Churches*, Vol. II (New York: Harper, 1960).
[4] G. R. Elton, *Reformation Europe, 1517–1559* (Cleveland: Meridian, 1963).

the first crystallization of the modern system

The outcome of the struggle between Reformation and Counter-Reformation was a double step toward pluralization and differentiation. The English-Dutch wing was more advanced, a harbinger for the future. Yet development within the Empire posed the crucial problem of integration *across* the Protestant–Roman Catholic line. Many historians of modern Europe have recognized only stalemated conflict here. Yet religious toleration has been extended to Roman Catholics in Protestant polities and even to Protestants in Roman Catholic polities, though generally without radical sacrifice of the establishment principle.

Religious pluralization was part of a process of differentiation between the cultural and societal systems that reduced the rigidity and diffuseness of their interpenetration. Religious *legitimation* of secular society was retained without committing governmental authority to the direct implementation or enforcement of religious goals.

The development of modern secular culture, with its high level of differentiation from society as a whole, has been important to the continuing interpenetration of religion and society. The focus of this development shifted northward in the seventeenth century to England and Holland but also to France and parts of Germany. *Relative* cultural decline in the heartland of the Counter-Reformation was clear after Galileo. The cultural importance of France indicated the equivocal nature, by Counter-Reformation standards, of its Roman Catholicism. Yet politically "reactionary" powers could be open to secular culture, as was Prussia under Frederick the Great. In general, secular culture found Protestantism more congenial than Roman Catholicism throughout this period.

The emergence of "sovereign" territorial states divided the Holy Roman Empire. They were first successfully established in France and England, which had been at best nominally part of the Empire at any time, and next in Spain, also on the geographical fringe. Then Prussia and Austria developed on the border of the "German" area, shifting the Empire's center of gravity toward the eastern frontier. In the central areas of the old Empire, territorial principalities proliferated largely through adherence of the princes to the Reformation.[5]

These developments also showed a certain cohesion of the European system, as all four of the leading political-territorial states were frontier units of the system. Both the northwest triangle and the Iberian peninsula faced the open sea and participated in the great maritime expansion of Europe. The latter also was partially occupied by the Moors whose occupation of much of the peninsula almost through the fifteenth century nurtured the militant authoritarianism of Hispanic Catholicism.[6]

[5] Geoffrey Barraclough, *The Origins of Modern Germany* (New York: Capricorn, 1963).
[6] Americo Castro, *The Structure of Spanish History* (Princeton: Princeton University Press, 1954).

the first crystallization of the modern system

Imperial "gravitation" toward the east was also associated with frontier conditions. The boundary between the Germanic and Slavic peoples had been unstable for many centuries—and was complicated even before the Reformation by relations between the Roman and Orthodox branches of Christianity. Hungary, Bohemia, and Poland were ethnically non-German but had become Roman Catholic. Especially after the fall of Byzantium the great Orthodox power was Russia, still peripheral to the Western system. The Germanic drive to organize and protect—and on occasion to dominate—the western Slavs eventuated in Hapsburg involvement with Hungary and Bohemia in an unstable multi- or non-national state. Incorporation of the non-German frontier peoples was complicated by Ottoman expansion, which remained a major threat until the late seventeenth century; Austria thus served as a defender of all *Christian* Europe.[7]

These developments at the borders of the European system "hollowed out" its center, especially in the Germany of "particularism," or *Kleinstaaterei*. The center failed to develop major territorial units, although a few like Saxony and Bavaria approached such status; numerous other "states" were very small indeed. These principalities did usually swallow up the free cities of the Empire, however. The independence of the urban bourgeois classes was undermined by monarchy, aristocracy, and officialdom, abetted by the devastation and disorganization of wars. This part of Europe, thus generally fell behind the Northwest in economic development and became a power vacuum before the ambitions of the stronger powers.[8]

We have been speaking deliberately of the "territorial" state, rather than of the "national" state. Only in England, France, and perhaps Scandinavia were ethnic community and governmental organization approximately coextensive. In Spain diverse local elements gradually developed a common language, at least among the upper classes. Prussia became more or less purely German, partly through Germanizing of large Slavic elements. Austria was conspicuously multiethnic, including large German, Slavic, and Hungarian elements. Switzerland achieved a special limited form of multiethnic political integration and religious pluralism. The small German states divided the ethnic "German nation" into numerous political units, leaving "Germany" even more disunited than "Italy."

Except in the northwest the lack of coincidence between ethnic group and territorial organization hindered the development of liberalizing societies based on independent and solidary societal communities as occurred in the northwest area. The main territorial units either lacked the

---

[7] Oscar Halecki, *The Limits and Divisions of European History* (Notre Dame, Ind.: University of Notre Dame Press, 1962).
[8] Bryce, *op. cit.*, and Barraclough, *op. cit.*

ethnic solidarity that can focus such communities or included small segments of larger ethnic communities for which their governments could not presume to speak. For political authorities in this precarious situation some form of fundamental religious legitimation was especially important. Their insecurity also contributed to political authoritarianism or "absolutism" and fear of concessions to popular participation in government. Their peoples were "subjects," rather than "citizens."

The religious fission of European society and the emergence of sovereign states precipitated severe crises that culminated in the seventeenth century. No functional equivalent of the old Empire appeared, and the matter of religious legitimation remained a serious weakness of the international system, as its power relations lacked adequate normative regulation.[9] This situation favored nearly chronic states of war and inhibited the constructive use of political power that could have emerged in a better-integrated collective system.

The Northwest

England, France, and Holland, each in a different way, took the lead in the power system of the seventeenth century. Dutch independence represented a major defeat for Spain. As the Austrians were heavily engaged against the Turks, Continental hegemony fell to the French. Though not yet a paramount force in Continental affairs, England did become the paramount maritime power during this century.

These three nations were the "spearhead" of early modernity. The most important developments occurred in their societal communities. The variations among the forms of the three societal communities were immense, but each contributed major innovations relative to national solidarity. In particular, the English conception of national identity provided a basis for a more clearly differentiated societal community.[10] This differentiation proceeded on three fronts—religious, political, and economic —each involving normative considerations. Legal innovations were thus critical, especially those that favored associational rather than bureaucratic potentials of the structure of national community. They were closely related to the emergence of parliamentarianism and more developed market economies.

Religion and Societal Community

As noted earlier, the Reformation deprived the "visible" church of its sacramental character. Subsequently, under the

[9] Bryce, op. cit., and Troeltsch, op. cit.
[10] See Hans Kohn, The Idea of Nationalism (New York: Macmillan, 1961).

the first crystallization of the modern system

formula *cuius regio, eius religio,* the tendency was to bring the church under tighter secular control, as there was no international Protestant church capable of reinforcing ecclesiastical independence. The Protestant churches thus tended to become state or "national" churches, and conformity was enforced through political authority.

A second, "Puritan" phase, based on Calvinism in England and Holland, led to religious pluralism *within* Protestantism, which contrasted sharply with the religious character of Prussia, several other Protestant German principalities, and Scandinavia.

In seventeenth-century England differentiation of the religious system from the societal community could not occur without heavy involvement in politics. The Long Parliament, the Civil War, the establishment of the Commonwealth, the Restoration, and the Revolution of 1688 involved not simply political issues but also the religious future of England and much else as well. English religious development involved not only the conversion of the crown to Protestantism but also a broadening of the Elizabethan measure of religious toleration.[11] The *political* legitimacy of the Nonconformists became firmly established, preventing a return to a politically established church with a monopoly of religious legitimacy. Furthermore, through Nonconformism, the Church of England was exposed to influences from the religious "left," which could have been repressed in a purely "state church" system. Indeed, the "evangelical" wing of the Church of England has been fundamental to subsequent English development.

Interestingly, the long and severe repression of Roman Catholicism in England [12] contributed to this outcome. Greater tolerance for Roman Catholicism during the eighteenth century might well have led to a second Stuart restoration and perhaps a serious attempt at a Roman Catholic reestablishment. The solidarity of a basically Protestant societal community and the relative absence of religious tension facilitated such developments as extension of the franchise. Had the English "right" been obliged to uphold the "true Church," as well as monarchy and aristrocracy, the strains would have been even more severe than they were, especially under the impact of the American and French Revolutions.[13]

Seventeenth-century Holland went considerably farther than England did in religious toleration. Over the long run, however, its religious constitution has proved less stable. A nineteenth-century Roman Catholic revival created a "columnar" structure among religious groups of approximately equal strength, thus introducing a severe religious rift into the

[11] W. K. Jordan, *The Development of Religious Toleration in England* (3 vols; Cambridge, Mass.: Harvard University Press, 1932–1940).
[12] The Catholic Emancipation Act was not passed until 1830.
[13] See R. R. Palmer, *The Age of the Democratic Revolution* (2 vols; Princeton: Princeton University Press, 1959 and 1964).

societal community.[14] Although the English Roman Catholic minority now has considerable strength, England has by and large escaped this problem.

France failed to "solve" its religious problem in an even more radical sense than Holland did. The outcome of the severe Reformation struggle was a Roman Catholic victory and suppression of the Protestant movement. Protestantism in France has never since involved more than small, though important, minorities. This weakness did not, however, secure the position of the Roman Catholic Church. *Secular* anticlericalism, based on the Enlightenment of the eighteenth century became a major political theme of the Revolution.[15] This conflict has persisted in France down to the present.

The basic French pattern has greatly influenced the definitions of religious legitimacy in other modern societies too, particularly in the Latin Catholic countries (including those of Latin America) but also in Germany and Eastern Europe. It has also contributed to the antireligious element in modern socialist movements, especially communism.

These European developments constitute a type of differentiation of the societal community and the religious system that in some respects offers an alternative to the pattern that emerged in seventeenth-century England and has reached its fullest development in the United States. The "Anglo-Saxon" pattern builds, however, on certain central religious traditions of Western society while accommodating societal solidarities that cut across the historic religious particularisms. Indeed, the range of religious commitments and solidarities that can be treated as compatible with societal membership has steadily broadened. Secular anticlericalism, however, especially in its communist version, remains closer to the formula of *cuius regio, eius religio*, with the implication that "nonconformists" must be excluded from the societal community.

The Polity and Societal Community

The societal community, as the main zone of integration between a normative structure and a collectivity structure in which certain crucial role loyalties of individuals are centered, has always involved both primary reliance on religious legitimation and unity under a clearly structured political authority. "Absolutism" represented a solution of the political aspects of the solidarity problems that arose from post-Reformation developments.[16] It required, however, that government—

---

14 S. M. Lipset and Stein Rokkan, "Introduction," in Lipset and Rokkan (eds.), *Cleavage Structures, Party Systems and Voter Alignment* (New York: Free Press, 1968).
15 See Palmer, *op. cit.*
16 See Max Beloff, *The Age of Absolutism, 1660–1815* (New York: Harper, 1962).

56

usually a monarchy—provide a central symbol on which loyalty could focus; such a symbol was enhanced by religious and ethnic unity. Indeed, religion and ethnic affiliation were the primary bases on which European society divided into territorial political units in early modern times,[17] with the general result that government and societal community were relatively undifferentiated. Nevertheless, in certain Western societies, there has been a tendency, under special conditions, to differentiate the two. England made an early and strong start in this direction, in contrast to France, an "absolutist" state in which government was identified with the societal community.

Ethnically, England, like France, had the problem of a "Celtic fringe," but only in Ireland was religion a seriously complicating factor. Ireland, where among the mass of the people Celtic ethnic affiliation coincided with Roman Catholicism and with class and geographical separation from England, was the prime area in which integration failed. Precisely in the critical period of the seventeenth century Cromwell fought bitter wars against the Irish, but the Roman Catholic Irish were never integrated into a "United Kingdom" as part of a unified societal community. Wales, though mainly Celtic, had a geographic disadvantage in maintaining its independence. It became predominantly Protestant, though more Nonconformist than was most of England, and posed no major problem of religious schism. The Scots developed an indubitable ethnic consciousness but fluctuated violently between Roman Catholicism and a more radical Protestantism than that of the English. The Scottish Stuarts became the focus of the Roman Catholic threat to the English religious constitution. Once the Protestant alternative had been consolidated, however, Scottish Presbyterianism became a major element in British Protestant denominational pluralism. Despite Ireland, therefore, Britain became relatively united ethnically, which contributed to its ability to afford religious pluralism within the bounds of Protestantism.[18]

Within a societal community, regional and ethnic differences are cut across by "vertical" axes of differentiation on the bases of power, prestige, and wealth. The geographical location of the center of societal organization—in Britain London—is a point of intersection.

A complex society requires substantial stratification, and it is all the more crucial in times of important innovation. As contributing to the innovative process is a function of the *kind* of stratification, we would expect to find important changes in stratification in the seventeenth century. Indeed, both the landed aristocracies that had developed from the feudal order and the urban patriciates were being transformed, and their relations with each other and with other groups were changing.

[17] Kohn, *op. cit.*
[18] *Ibid.*

the first crystallization of the modern system

The landed aristocracies were the most important upper class, providing the support in prestige for the early development of modern territorial monarchies.[19] The monarch was generally not only the chief of state but also the "first gentleman" of his society, the apex of a complex structured hierarchy of social prestige. The aristocracy itself was a seamless web of lineages, an affinal collectivity bound by intermarriage and eligibility for intermarriage.[20]

Aristocratic lineages have tended to be anchored in local interest structures, especially in land. Historic landed proprietorship was, however, a diffuse superiority status, including not only ownership but also elements of political control and social ascendance.

The rise of the early modern state reduced the political power of particularistically defined aristocratic subgroups, especially their autonomous territorial and military jurisdiction, in favor of a prestige position that supported the monarchy.[21] Adequate economic support for those prestige positions rested largely in land ownership. In predominantly rural areas, therefore, economic elements were not radically different from a more diffuse social matrix, the apex of which was local aristocracy.[22]

Under feudal conditions the whole aristocracy of Europe was, in principle, a single "seamless web." This unity was incompatible, however, with division into national states. Religious differences resulting from the Reformation created barriers to intermarriage and helped to contain the aristocracy supporting a prince within *eius religio*, but it did not eliminate the problem. In England, since the Tudor period "foreign" dynasties have been more the rule than the exception: the Scottish Stuarts, the Dutch House of Orange, and the German Hanoverians. Had this cosmopolitanism extended to all the aristocracy, it would have impeded the consolidation of ethnic-national identities. It is important, then, that England and France, the two leading national states, split on religious and linguistic lines so that their aristocracies became basically distinct from each other—and from others.

Along with the "nationalization" of the aristocracy, the integration of top political authority with aristocracy was a primary factor in enabling royal governments to establish their authority over national societal communities.[23] This possibility in turn depended largely upon the military functions of aristocracies.

[19] See Palmer, *op. cit.*, and Beloff, *op. cit.*
[20] This conception of "affinal collectivity" has been much influenced by the author's discussions with Charles D. Ackerman.
[21] Palmer, *op. cit.*, and Beloff, *op. cit.*
[22] See Barrington Moore, Jr., *Social Origins of Dictatorship and Democracy: Lord and Peasant in the Making of the Modern World* (Boston: Beacon, 1966).
[23] Beloff, *op. cit.*, and John B. Wolf, *The Emergence of the Great Powers* (New York: Harper, 1962).

58

The process of differentiation between government and societal community was also focused on the relations between monarchy and aristocracy, as shown by the deep conflicts of interest between the two. The political power institutionalized in *specific* aristocratic status was greatly lessened. Yet the new total power position of aristocracies varied greatly, as the examples of England and France show.

Broadly speaking, the differentiation occurred in France in such a way as to leave the aristocracy overwhelmingly dependent upon its social prestige. On the whole, it was deprived not only of the exercise of political power but also of the functions of contributing major contingent support to political authority and of exerting a major influence over governmental policy.[24] The sign of this outcome was the brilliant court of Versailles. Centralization at the court loosened the attachment of the aristocracy to their local communities, depriving them of local political power, which in turn facilitated the encroachment of the central government on local affairs.[25]

These remarks apply most directly to the older, more 'feudal" aristocracy, the *noblesse d'épée*. The position of the newer aristocracy relatively recently risen from bourgeois origins and based predominantly on legal training, reinforced the integration of aristocracy and crown. The legal profession was closely associated with the crown through public offices merging administrative and judicial components. As legal officials, the French lawyers stood between the crown and both the older aristocracy and the bourgeoisie. There was considerable upward mobility through these intermediate circles, partly through the sale of offices. Yet the upwardly mobile elements generally sought to attain the status of nobility and to make their offices hereditary.[26]

Economically the *noblesse de robe* was primarily dependent upon the crown both for various perquisites of its offices and, to the extent that it held land, for enforcement of feudal dues and obligations upon the peasantry. It lacked an independent economic base comparable to that of the English landed gentry.

The Church was closely integrated into this system. More than in England, high clerical offices went to members of aristocratic lineages. Furthermore, there was no equivalent of English Protestant Nonconformism. This absence contributed to the militant anticlerricalism of the Revolutionary opposition to the ancien régime. There was a collegial aspect to the *noblesse*, in the form of the *parlements*. In contrast to the British parliamentary system, however, the *parlements* were considerably

---

[24] Franklin L. Ford, *Robe and Sword: The Regrouping of the French Aristocracy After Louis XIV* (Cambridge, Mass.: Harvard University Press, 1953).
[25] *Ibid.*
[26] Palmer, *op. cit.*

more judicial and administrative than legislative. Furthermore, there was no one central *parlement* but a whole series of regional *parlements*. The *parlement* of Paris had only the precedence of primus inter pares, rather than the exclusive position occupied by the Parliament of Westminster.

The deprivation of political power among the French aristocracy seems related to the group's ambivalent role in the eighteenth century. On one hand, it developed a "snobbish" exclusiveness vis-à-vis all "bourgeois" elements, many of whom had surpassed its members in political position, wealth, and cultivation.[27] On the other hand, it was particularly prominent as a sponsor of modernizing cultural movements, notably in "philosophy," and thus contributed crucially to the French Enlightenment.[28] Both these developments rendered problematic the position of the French aristocracy as the legitimate élite of the societal community. The aristocracy's dependence on the monarchy for its *social* prestige was combined with dissociation from the rest of the societal community in terms of both government power and the cultural "mediocrity" of the common man. The whole structure of crown, the two *noblesses*, and the Church was placed against the bourgeoisie and all the other classes,[29] thus fostering the split in French society that erupted in the Revolution.

England developed differently as it departed from the initial symbiosis between government and aristocracy. Instead of "disfranchising" the aristocracy, the monarchy became its "creature." The executive functions of government and the societal community underwent a process of differentiation focused on the "support system," [30] which articulated the two. This system was centered in Parliament. In contrast to France, Parliament had consolidated a position of "real power" by 1688.

This power did not mean, however, "government by aristocracy," the simple obverse of the French solution. First, the national aristocracy was too diffuse actually to "govern"—one reason why both the Stuarts and Cromwell successfully advocated strong executive authority. Eventually there developed the system of cabinet government under a constitutional monarch who "reigned" but did not govern. Second, there was the special character of the British aristocracy. Primogeniture in England, reinforced by entail, had tended to keep estates intact over generations and to produce continuous social gradations between the titled nobility

<hr/>

[27] Elinor Barber, *The Bourgeoisie in Eighteenth Century France* (Princeton: Princeton University Press, 1955).

[28] Palmer, *op. cit.*

[29] See especially Moore, *op. cit.*, and Ford, *op. cit.*

[30] Talcott Parsons, "The Political Aspects of Social Structure and Process," in David Easton (ed.), *Varieties of Political Theory* (Englewood Cliffs, N.J.: Prentice-Hall, 1966). Reprinted in *Politics and Social Structure* (New York: Free Press, 1969) Chapter 13.

the first crystallization of the modern system

and their untitled collaterals, the "gentry," who might or might not be closely related to titled families. This system favored both upward mobility into the aristocracy and indefinite extension of the status of "gentleman" downward from the titled nobility.

The status of the gentry became formalized in the House of Commons. As there were too many gentlemen for the Commons to be simply an assembly of an estate of the realm, as was the House of Lords (to which every peer belonged), it became a *representative* body.[31] As the Commons became increasingly important relative to the Lords, the distinction between those actually exercising political power and their constituencies became important. The gentry as a whole became a constituency, not a component, of government.

During the earlier period the aristocracy, as a major component of the societal community, constituted the most active element in the support system of government yet remained relatively independent of governmental organization. Furthermore, representative participation in government facilitated the gradual emergence of a party system under which elements of society could influence the policies and selection of active executive leadership somewhat responsive to the constituencies.[32]

The second main type of inherited privilege was that of the urban upper class, which rested primarily on commerce. Because the rural sector of the economy was generally still predominant, territorial consolidation under the monarchies gave primacy to rural interests and was less favorable to urban upper groups: a major reason why the most highly urbanized areas were for a long time not incorporated in territorial monarchies but defended the "free city" pattern.

Holland was an exception. In winning its independence from Spain, it became primarily a federation of urban communities led by merchant groups. It experienced considerable difficulty in integrating its rural areas, however, and lacked the cohesion of its rivals. Yet, in avoiding the social dominance of a landed aristocracy, it set an important example for future development.

England's middle position facilitated a synthesis. The representative character of the House of Commons provided machinery for the political involvement of important bourgeoise groups, and the line between them and the untitled gentry did not become rigid as in France.[33] This flexibility

[31] C. H. McIlwain, *The High Court of Parliament* (New Haven: Yale University Press, 1910); and F. W. Maitland, *The Constitutional History of England* (Cambridge, Eng.: Cambridge University Press, 1908).

[32] See Lewis Namier, *England in the Age of the American Revolution* (2nd ed.; London: Macmillan, 1961).

[33] See Archibald S. Foord, *His Majesty's Opposition 1714–1830* (Oxford: Oxford University Press, 1964).

the first crystallization of the modern system

was in turn facilitated by the relatively pluralistic political system including the crown, the City of London, and the aristocracy, itself divided between nobility and gentry.

This pluralism made relatively easy the inclusion of other emerging elements in the societal community. Indeed the constituency of the House of Commons was gradually extended not only to the boroughs but in the nineteenth century to a broad mass electorate as well. By the late seventeenth century England had both a relatively firmly integrated national state and a relatively pluralistic support system, which favored future democratization in a step-by-step manner, rather than through abrupt revolutionary change.

These political circumstances were strongly reinforced by the English religious constitution and by development of the common law. Universalistic legal principles and the broad conception of the "rule of law," as distinguished from arbitrary authority, were institutionalized in legal systems practically all over Europe after the Renaissance, building on Roman traditions. Yet the common law was distinctive in three important and related ways.[34] First was judicial independence from the crown, which came to a head with the ultimately successful struggle of Chief Justice Coke against James I.[35] Second was the closely corporate character of the legal profession, organized about the Inns of Court. Third was the emphasis upon legal embodiment of private rights and interests, sometimes against the privileges of government, sometimes in areas outside the normal range of governmental concern.[36] This process had two aspects. The first involved the "rights of Englishmen," including habeas corpus, fair trial and counsel, the protection of homes against arbitrary search, and ultimately free speech, assembly, and the like. The second involved property and contract, essential foundations of the industrial revolution. Coke's attack on the "monopolies" established by royal charter was of great significance, a legal precursor of Adam Smith's attack on mercantilism.

English legal developments contributed substantially to differentiating government from the societal community. Law became less an instrument of government and more a mediating "interface" between the two. It had to serve the needs of government but was sufficiently independent to serve pluralistic private needs as well. Government was thus placed in the dual position of defining and enforcing certain legally embodied restrictions on its own powers.

[34] See Maitland, *op. cit.*, and F. W. Maitland, *English Law and the Renaissance* (Cambridge, Eng.: Cambridge University Press, 1901).
[35] Maitland, *English Law and the Renaissance*, McIlwain, *op. cit.*, and Roscoe Pound, *The Spirit of the Common Law* (Boston: Beacon, 1963).
[36] Pound, *op. cit.*

62

the first crystallization of the modern system

The legal profession came to occupy an interstitial status. It became established that judges, even in the exercise of the judicial powers of the House of Lords, should be professional lawyers. Both judges and barristers, the core of the legal profession, however, served mainly private clients, which might include government agencies.

Members of the legal profession—including judges—became the primary guardians of the rights of the general public, especially "civil" rights [37] and those of property, contract, and torts.[38] The independence of the judiciary and the bar seems also to have been related to the emergence of the second main branch of the British legal profession, the solicitors, who lacked the privilege of pleading in court but were the principal legal advisers to groups of all sorts. Through the solicitors the legal system penetrated the pluralistic structure of interest groups; through the bar and judiciary it maintained its delicate relation to government. The Inns of Court were in many ways reminiscent of medieval guilds. They resisted the "streamlining" of law that occurred on the Continent, the formalization of university training, the appointment of the most influential group of lawyers as civil servants, and an examination system to guarantee competence.

Although judges were public officials, they were also lawyers trained in an extragovernmental profession and *responsible* to the traditions of the common law. The barristers and solicitors, though private professional practitioners, also had public prerogatives and responsibilities. Furthermore, the adversary system acquired a special status. More than on the Continent, legal actions were conducted between private parties, each represented by counsel,before a judge and often heard by a jury under *procedural* rules. The judge tended to become an umpire rather than a decision maker. Furthermore, the courts themselves shaped law, especially in rendering decisions and setting precedents relatively independently of royal decrees and acts of Parliament.

The English system left the boundaries of the legal system quite open, permitting tentative approaches to consensus before full "legalization" of a norm and its enforcement by governmental authority were reached. Appeals to collective solidarity, moral standards, and practicality thus had a place in the system other than through high-level policy determination.

Continental legal systems differed from that of England, despite

[37] See T. H. Marshall, *Class, Citizenship, and Social Development* (Garden City, N.Y.: Anchor, 1965).

[38] In Durkheim's terms, this development indicated a new emphasis on "restitutive" over "repressive" law. See Émile Durkheim, *The Division of Labor in Society* (London: Macmillan, 1933).

common origins and some common features. The new Continental monarchies tended to maintain the Roman legal tradition and its emphasis on the "unitary" authority of the state.[39] This tradition tended to make civil law the instrument of government by bringing the dominant group of legally trained people into governmental service, often as the core of the developing civil services.[40] Civil administration was thus differentiated from the military, which remained largely in the hands of the aristocracies. The Continental legal systems generally promoted the effectiveness of government more adequately than did the British one,[41] yet the latter made possible a more advanced state of differentiation and integration between government and the societal community.

The Economy and Societal Community

The crucial economic developments in England during the sixteenth and seventeenth centuries centered on the enclosure movement and its complex aftermath. Most important was the growth of commercial farming, oriented toward markets, as distinct from the nearly subsistence farming of the medieval type, under which the sale of produce extended only to neighboring towns.[42] The major break with the old system was the development of a large export trade with the wool manufacturers of Flanders and Italy. The increase in large-scale sheep raising required displacement of considerable elements of the tenant population, for sheep raising was less labor-intensive than was crop raising and was hindered by the traditional open-field system of manorial agriculture.

Many of the gentry and even noble landowners actively promoted the change, either becoming commercial farmers themselves or renting their lands to commercial tenants. The secular owners of previously ecclesiastical lands, especially of monasteries that had been dissolved, were less traditional in estate management than the Church had been. Many members of the gentry also engaged, directly or through agents, in non-agricultural economic enterprise, particularly various commercial ventures. The general process was by no means complete by the end of the seventeenth century, but, along with the other factors that we have reviewed, it had already had two major consequences.

First, the proportion of peasants who were individual tenants, or even independent proprietors, had diminished. Instead, agricultural laborers

---

39 See the discussion in Talcott Parsons, *Societies: Evolutionary and Comparative Perspectives* (Englewood Cliffs, N.J.: Prentice-Hall, 1966).

40 Ford, *op. cit.*

41 This aspect was emphasized by Weber; see Max Rheinstein (ed.), *Max Weber on Law in Economy and Society* (Cambridge, Mass.: Harvard University Press, 1954).

42 Karl Polanyi, *The Great Transformation* (New York: Beacon, 1957).

the first crystallization of the modern system

appeared,[43] and the surplus rural population tended to leave the country-side and gradually became a laboring class in the towns. A new concern with indigence and vagabondage emerged [44] in response to the dislocations and human suffering that they entailed; from then on, the "Poor Laws" were to be a prominent issue. The "peasant class" was sufficiently weakened so that struggles over its rights and position were not as prominent in England as in France.[45]

Second, the land-owning classes tended to become "defeudalized." Their economic position came to depend increasingly upon the market success of their farming and other enterprises rather than upon the enforcement of feudal obligations on a peasant class. This increased the productivity of agriculture, but it also gave the aristocracy more economical flexibility, enabling it to incorporate increasingly large commercial and then industrial elements.[46] This relaxation created a common interest and a partial fusion with the predominantly urban upper classes, but certainly partly at the expense of the peasantry.

The situation in France was almost the reverse. There the aristocracy was economically dependent upon the crown.[47] Because of the independence of the French Church from Rome, the crown had far-reaching control of ecclesiastical appointments, which, along with military commissions and the sale of civil offices, it used to fortify the loyalty of important aristocratic elements. In addition, the aristocracy was dependent upon priveleged exemptions from taxes and upon enforcement of obligations upon the peasantry.[48] French agricultural traditions were thus not conducive to reorganization in the interest of productivity. The peasantry remained relatively intact and in potentially sharp conflict with the land-owning class, which helped to entrench the *combination* of monarchy, aristocracy, and Church further under the ancien régime,[49] as well as fostering peasant support for the Revolution, though in some circumstances, as in the Vendée, the peasants did swing to the other side.[50] Furthermore, in France there was little reason for urban groups to support the old regime. In Holland aristocracy was much weaker, but there were

---

[43] An interesting reflection of the situation is that the classical economists, particularly Ricardo, generally took commercial agriculture as a paradigmatic use in their analyses. It was the agricultural laborer, the employee of a commercial farmer, who was primarily discussed in connection with wage theory.

[44] *Ibid.*

[45] Moore, *op. cit.*

[46] *Ibid.*

[47] Ford, *op. cit.*, and Moore, *op. cit.*

[48] Moore, *op. cit.*; see also Georges Lefebvre, *The Coming of the French Revolution* (New York: Vintage, 1960).

[49] Palmer, *op. cit.*

[50] Moore, *op. cit.*; and Charles Tilly, *The Vendée* (Cambridge, Mass.: Harvard University Press, 1964).

the first crystallization of the modern system

important conflicts of interest between the commercial urban groups and the rural society of the "hinterland." [51]

The export trade in wool supported the new level of English commercial activity. It strengthened urban commercial interests centered in London, the seat of government, as well as the commercial and financial center and a major port. The "putting-out system" [52] between spinners and weavers of wool in the countryside and the wool merchants provided an escape from the restrictive rules of the urban guilds. Merchants in the towns "staked" countryside weavers who had home looms with yarn, collected the finished cloth, and sent it to London merchants for export. This system provided yet another bridge of economic interest between the land-owning gentry and the upper groups in the towns.

The differentiation engendered by these economic changes was similar to the kind that emerged between governmental organization and societal community. The medieval differentiation between town and country involved only very partial economic differentiation. Its basis is the distinction between primary or "extractive" production (notably agriculture) and trade and manufacture (mostly handicrafts) involved the economic division of labor but extended economic and other functions through *whole communities*. A rural village was thus an agricultural unit, and a neighboring town was a unit for the provision of manufactured goods. Other functions, like government, were centralized and could not be spread equally through all the small community units.

The "squires" long held much of the local power, and the gentry contributed the "social" leaders of "county society." The employment of tenant farmers by owners, however, differentiated their own functions as social and political leaders in the local community from those of economic production in which their land was a factor of production. When farms became more specifically economic enterprises, agricultural laborers and tenant farmers were employed in something closer to modern occupational roles than the heriditary status of villein had been, and the standards of success for enterprise became linked to solvency through market operations. Through the market, land owners established connections with groups outside their own rural communities, especially merchants and "putting-out" entrepreneurs. This trend proliferated through specific markets and extended economic relations that did not coincide with relations of other sorts, for example citizenship in local communities. Although the participants in the economic system could thus be divided generally into an "agricultural interest," a "mercantile interest," and, increasingly, a "manufacturing interest," it became more and more difficult to identify these interests

[51] Palmer, *op. cit.*
[52] See Edwin F. Gay, "Putting-Out System," in *Encyclopedia of the Social Sciences* (New York: Macmillan, 1934).

66
the first crystallization of the modern system

with whole communities rather than with differentiated units within communities.

Conclusion

Our major thesis has been that England had become by the end of the seventeenth century the most highly differentiated society in the European system, having advanced farther in this direction than had any previous society. Taking the societal community as our main point of reference, we have discussed the differentiation of religion, government, and economy from it.

First, the combination of a Protestant establishment with significant toleration and denominational pluralism broke the traditional European fusion of religion and government with the societal community. Not only was English government obligated to accord major rights to religious nonconformists, but also citizenship in the societal community was no longer bound to traditional religious conformity. This separation entailed both a new mode of integration and greater differentiation, in that the acceptable societal community was no longer confined to the coreligionists of the king (*eius religio*) but *included* Protestant nonconformists as well.

These developments involved generalization of the value level of the pattern-maintenance system in English society in two respects. First, the basis of value consensus had to be "moral," in the sense of being more general than any one denominational position would be. The Reformation and the splintering of Protestantism threatened the solidarity of the societal community. In England denominational religious commitment was, however, differentiated from moral consensus at the societal level. Second, there emerged a common commitment to the value of rational knowledge of the world, partly but not wholly because of its practical utility. Although not without strain, philosophy and science *as such*— not only, for example, Anglican philosophy and science—came to be regarded as "good things," supported across the religious spectrum, including Roman Catholicism.

Given the establishment of a "national" community, two main mechanisms of differentiation between the societal community and government developed. One was a government in which highly influential elements of the societal community were constituents of representative bodies rather than members of government; the critical role was played by the House of Commons. The second main mechanism was the law. More than any other legal system, English law drew a clear distinction between the status of member in the societal community with rights that the government was obligated to observe and the status of "subject" of the king as chief of government.

This differentiation was reinforced by the trend of relations between

the first crystallization of the modern system

aristocracy and government in England. Much of the English aristocracy became an active political *constituency* of government, instead of remaining part of the undifferentiated structure of government without an opportunity to play a decisive part in it. This pattern permitted later extension, so that larger groups could gain inclusion in the political aspect of citizenship.[53]

The consolidation of the common law and the supremacy of Parliament in government were closely connected with Puritanism and the special religious settlement that emerged in England.[54] Denominational and political pluralism expressed the differentiation of the societal community from religious collectivities and governmental organization. Both aspects involved a process of inclusion associated with that of differentiation. Legitimate status of full membership in the societal community was accorded to religious dissenters and to political opponents of the group currently in office as long as they constituted a "loyal opposition." The legal system, both in its normative content and in its structural independence, was a primary mechanism regulating the boundary relations among these differentiated elements. It is crucial that there were *legally* institutionalized rights of religious and political dissent. England never resorted to a written constitution that would formally bind the "crown in Parliament" as the theoretical sovereign of the realm; nor were the courts of law ever accorded the power of judicial review, in the sense of authorization to declare acts of Parliament unconstitutional. Nevertheless, the record confirms the essential effectiveness of the legal institutionalization of "constitutional" limitations upon the powers of government, despite the close relation between government and the coercive sanctions of the courts.

The differentiation of societal community and economy focussed on the "commercialization" of agriculture, especially as it affected the landed interests of the gentry. Generally rural communities have undifferentiated ascriptive structures particularly resistant to modernization. The orientation of English agriculture to the market, however, created commercial interest that linked the rural communities "horizontally" with the towns, rather than "vertically" with a feudal type of aristocratic governmental hierarchy, and reduced the severity of the "peasant problem."

In the towns a parallel process of differentiation was breaking down the particularism of the guild system. As England was on the whole less urbanized than were some areas of the Continent, it was important that a major rural interest favored this differentiating process. The primary *institutional* foundations of a differentiated market economy were laid in England well before the mechanical inventions and other innovations of

[53] Marshall, *op. cit.*
[54] See David Little, *Religion, Law, and Order* (New York: Harper and Row, 1969).

the first crystallization of the modern system

the industrial revolution. The Puritan influence was very important as well, perhaps especially in the orientations of the innovative merchant groups but also among the gentry, many of whom were Puritans.

The economic phase of English development seems also to have promoted pluralism in the community structure. The processes of differentiation, which occurred within both rural and urban communities, strengthened a community of economic interests that cut across the old distinction. This trend was important above all in view of the political power of the landed classes. Economic differentiation provided a basis on which future urban groups could be included in a single solidary system. Rural-urban conflicts were not as severe in England as elsewhere in subsequent periods; compared with the situation in France, conflict between the bourgeoisie and the landed aristocracy was mild.

The process of adaptive upgrading was most obviously associated with economic development. Not only in England, but also in the whole northwestern triangle, the seventeenth century was a period of substantial economic advance. There were progressive increases in the "extent of the market," both internally and externally, for each political unit.

Though within societies as social systems adaptive capacity is focussed in the economic sphere, it is affected by developments in both the cultural and personality systems. On the cultural side, the most conspicuous process of upgrading was the general development of secular culture, with its emphasis upon cognitive rationality in philosophy and science. This trend was furthered in Holland and England by the values of ascetic Protestantism.[55] Although the growth of cognitive and rational culture had not yet had primary consequences for the structure of society, it had an impact. After Newton and Locke, for example, cultural leaders could not ignore the implications of the new science and philosophy for a vast range of concerns; they were equipped with a new level of adaptive resources.

The central development related to the adaptive aspect of personality was the emphasis of ascetic Protestantism upon the orientational complex that Weber called "worldly asceticism." It enhanced motivation to achievement in "worldly callings." The "situation" for giving meaning to such achievement was culturally "defined" as "this-worldly," rather than as "other-worldly," oriented toward the building of the good society and not only toward the salvation of souls in the afterlife. It was universalistic and

---

[55] Merton's analysis of the relations of Puritanism and science in England has been not "refuted" but merely qualified by recent research. See Robert K. Merton, "Science, Technology and Society in Seventeenth Century England," *Osiris*, 4 (1938) reprinted in *Social Theory and Social Structure*, Chapter 18, (rev. ed.; Glencoe, Ill.: Free Press, 1957); see also Joseph Ben-David, *The Sociology of Science* (Englewood Cliffs, N.J.: Prentice-Hall, 1971).

innovative in that the mandate for achievement was applicable to all men and was to build a new "kingdom," not to perpetuate tradition.

Encouragement of this type of personal orientation had selective effects in different spheres. One was to enhance the relevance of scientific investigation. Another was the broad pressure for a certain type of individualism in English law.[56] There was, however, a special connection with the economic sphere, through market relations. This connection did not develop primarily, as has so persistently been alleged, because the market opened the doors to "self-interest" or "materialism." Rather, it developed because the market mechanism constituted the first massive institutional context within which it was possible to isolate individual achievements and contributions from a diffuse matrix of irrelevant ties. The market represented a differentiation of the social structure to the point at which differential opportunity, evaluation of individual contributions, and in some sense proportional rewards were possible on a wider scale than ever before. This possibility seems to us the primary significance of the connection between the Protestant Ethic of individual achievement and its expression in market activity, made famous by Weber.[57]

[56] Little, op. cit.

[57] The connection between Protestant religious orientations and modern economic ethics has long been the subject of academic debate. The classics of the debate are Max Weber, The Protestant Ethic and the Spirit of Capitalism (New York: Scribner, 1958); and R. H. Tawney, Religion and the Rise of Capitalism (New York: Mentor, Books, 1947). See also R. W. Green (ed.), Protestantism and Capitalism (Boston: Heath, 1959); and Talcott Parsons, "Richard Henry Tawney," American Sociological Review (December 1962).

the first crystallization of the modern system

counterpoint
and further
development:
the age of
revolutions
five

The Differentiation of Europe
in the Age of Revolutions

The Counter-Reformation societies tended drastically to "freeze" the process of differentiation, as we indicated in the last chapter, primarily because of the relations between their political regimes and a very defensive Church. Not only Protestantism but also many modernizing trends had to be opposed, especially those that might foster the independence of universalistically oriented units from the core structure of government, aristocracy, and church. These units included the "business" elements, those advocating more extensive and more democratic political participation, and "intellectual" groups, which by the eighteenth century were viewed with great suspicion by the authorities. The heartland of the Counter-Reformation, the Italian states and the papacy, served a primarily pattern-maintenance function in the general European system.

Spain became the most militant spokesman for the pre-Reformation order of society, often seeming "more Catholic than the Pope." In its secular social structure, Spain offered perhaps the prime example of a

71

major society frozen at an early modern level. In many respects its intransigent traditionalism isolated it from the rest of Europe.[1]

Austria, held together by royal and aristocratic intermarriage and Roman Catholic allegiance, contrasted sharply with Spain in its handling of ethnic heterogeneity. Although at first committed to the Counter-Reformation, the Austrian Habsburgs later accepted a limited religious pluralism established by the settlement of 1648. They were thus anachronistic in their lack of concern with political nationality, but they played an important integrative role by maintaining a large political structure that became first ethnically and then religiously pluralistic.[2] That the Empire eventually disintegrated under the centrifugal forces of nationalism does not negate its importance over a long transitional period. Indeed, as late as the Holy Alliance, Austria was the focus of conservative integrationism in Europe. Furthermore, it played an important role in mediating Russia's entry into the European system, a role encouraged by mutual conflict with Napoleonic France.

The particularistic area of Germany resembled the Counter-Reformation center despite its religious diversity. Its small states were necessarily on the defensive also, threatened as they were with absorption by their larger neighbors. As in the Italian states, major structural innovations were inhibited.[3]

The Prussian role in the European system, conditioned by the open eastern frontier, crystallized on the basis of a special variant of the Protestant pattern. The Hohenzollern rulers had converted to Calvinism, whereas the bulk of the population adhered to Lutheranism. What emerged was a special form of the Protestant "national church" that amalgamated the two elements.[4] Calvinism, within the activist pattern of ascetic Protestantism, postulated the general dominance in the community of a religious élite, the predestined elect, setting it above even the faithful Protestant common people. It was also strongly collectivist in that it conceived any Calvinist community to be founded upon its religiously ordained mission. This orientation—activist, authoritarian, and collectivist—well fitted the Prussian monarchy as a boundary unit seeking to expand at the cost of the Slavs. Furthermore, it dovetailed with the Lutheran emphasis on the legitimacy of duly constituted authority in maintaining a given order and in checking disorder, which might include almost any major change.

[1] Americo Castro, *The Structure of Spanish History* (Princeton: Princeton University Press, 1954).

[2] James Bryce, *The Holy Roman Empire* (rev. ed.; London: Macmillan, 1904).

[3] Geoffrey Barraclough, *The Origins of Modern Germany* (New York: Capricorn, 1963).

[4] Christine Kayser, "Calvinism and German Political Life," Unpublished doctoral dissertation, Radcliffe College, 1961.

counterpoint and further development: the age of revolutions

Calvinism was admirably suited to a forcible governing class, Lutheranism to its subjects. Along with the general unsettlement of any changing frontier community, this religious situation helps to explain Prussian advances in rationalizing both military and civil administration.

Like most of Continental Europe, Prussia was organized about a land-owning aristocracy, the Junkers. The Junkers did not become a parliamentary opposition to royal absolutism as had the English gentry; instead they were a primary support of the monarchy, particularly in a military capacity. As in England, however, they transformed their traditional estates into commercial farming operations oriented toward the export of grain. The changes nonetheless incorporated the old rigid class structure, which was strengthened when the agricultural workers who migrated to the new industries were replaced largely by Polish laborers.[5]

Before the nineteenth century, Prussia's most important advances were in governmental effectiveness; in both military and civil bureaucratic administration it set new standards for Europe.[6] Certainly Prussia's military record, considering its size and resources, made it the Sparta of modern Europe. All classes in its hierarchically organized population came to accept a stringent conception of duty, much like the one formulated by Kant, but in this instance duty specifically to the state. The state managed to combine a relatively amenable lower group, a traditionally military landed gentry, and a not very large or strong but very urban-oriented upper *Bürgertum* in a highly effective operating organization.[7] Gradually, it took advantage of the "liberal-national" movements in the German world, rather than being threatened by them, a trend culminating in the career of Bismarck.

Prussia's effectiveness as a sovereign state enabled it to extend its political domination over other territories; it gained control of practically all northern Germany, foreshadowing the exclusion of Austria from leadership in the unification of Germany. When the German Empire was constituted in 1871, it included a large Roman Catholic minority (nearly one-third of the population), the reverse of the settlement of 1648, which had included a Protestant minority in the old Roman Catholic Empire.[8] Prussia's expansion into other parts of Germany, however, produced severe strains in the societal community, the religious diversity of which was not yet adequately integrated in a pluralistic structure.

Almost coincidentally with Prussia's expansion, the new Germany

[5] See the account of Weber's early researches in Reinhard Bendix, *Max Weber: An Intellectual Portrait* (Garden City, N.Y.: Anchor, 1962); see also Reinhard Bendix, *Nation-Building and Citizenship* (New York: Wiley, 1964), Chapters 4, 6.

[6] Hans Rosenberg, *Bureaucracy, Aristocracy, and Autocracy: The Prussian Experience, 1660–1815* (Cambridge, Mass.: Harvard University Press, 1958).

[7] *Ibid.*

[8] Barraclough, *op. cit.*

became the primary site of the second major phase of the Industrial Revolution. The buildup that established the political position of imperial Germany did not immediately include any major economic advance beyond that of early modern Europe generally. The major change came surprisingly slowly,[9] considering how long the British example had been available. Furthermore, it centered not in the main areas of Prussian "efficiency" but in the territories about the Rhineland, which were generally more Roman Catholic than Protestant.[10]

Until the spread of the industrial revolution to the Continent, Britain, Prussia, and France had been in the forefront of change. In the differentiation of the European system as a whole, we may attribute primacy of goal-attaining functions to the Northwest, for the most important new institutional developments and structural differentiation were emerging there. These processes increased the adaptive capacity of the system, particularly in economic terms and in England.

For this same period, we may assign primacy of the more general adaptive function to Prussia. It had become the most important stabilizer of Europe's open eastern frontier. Furthermore, it had pioneered in the development of instrumentally effective collective organization, a generalized resource that has since been diffused throughout all functional sectors of modern societies.

The Industrial Revolution

The late eighteenth century saw the beginning of the two developments marking the transition from the early phase of Western modernity to the one that has crystallized in the mid-twentieth century. These changes are usually called the industrial revolution and the democratic revolution. The former began in Great Britain, whereas the latter erupted in France in 1789.

The emergence of these developments in the northwest sector of Europe capped the main developmental trends of the earlier period. As do all major structural changes, they occasioned severe strains where they emerged and even more severe strains when they spread into areas less well prepared for them.

The main developmental trend after the Reformation stressed, under an activist value system, the adaptive and integrative capacities of societies, which involved new orders of differentiation and increased organic solidarity in Durkheim's sense. The industrial revolution was part of this trend, in that vast increases in economic productivity entailed immense extension of the division of labor in the social sense. As we have em-

[9] See David Landes, *The Rise of Capitalism* (New York: Macmillan, 1966).
[10] See Rainer Baum, "Values and Uneven Political Development in Imperial Germany," unpublished doctoral dissertation, Harvard University, 1967.

74

phasized, such extensions in differentiation produce a functional need for new integrative structures and mechanisms. The democratic revolution involved primarily the integrative aspect of the societies; it focused on the political meaning of membership in the societal community and thus on the justification of inequalities in wealth and, more important, in political authority and social privilege.

Our primary interest in the industrial revolution is not in its technological and strictly economic aspects but in associated changes in social structure. It should be noted, however, that the technological changes had revolutionary economic effects. They made possible extremely large cost savings, lower prices, and the development of many new products.[11] In England the process began in the cotton-textile industry and spread to the "heavier" industries, whereas on the Continent and in the United States the main development broadly coincided with the spread of the railroads.[12]

The structural key to the industrial revolution is the extension of the market system and of the attendant differentiation in the economic sector of the social structure. The market system itself, however, did not undergo a sudden revolution but only a long and continuous evolution. The distinctive prosperity of England and Holland especially, but also of France, before the new inventions undoubtedly resulted from the development of their market systems, which in turn depended upon legal and political security and legal frameworks based on property and contract, which favored the extension of commercial enterprise. English and Dutch prosperity was also a function of both relatively light governmental pressures on economic resources, especially the absence of large standing armies, and of an absence of the sharp aristocratic objections to "trade" that prevailed in most Continental countries.

Before the industrial revolution the most developed sector of the market system was finished commodities, generally luxury goods.[13] The most important exception in England was the production for export first of wool, then of woolen cloth. In some areas grain was an important market commodity, but most foodstuffs and articles of general consumption entered the market system only within local limits, if at all. Typical was the exchange of foodstuffs grown in the immediate locality for handicrafts of a "market" town.[14]

From this focus the market system could spread in several directions. From the consumer product, it could extend "back" into earlier stages of

[11] There is an enormous literature on these problems. Landes, *op. cit.*, is a thorough and particularly illuminating survey.
[12] J. H. Clapham, *Economic Development of France and Germany, 1815–1914* (Cambridge, Mass.: Cambridge University Press, 1963).
[13] See Max Weber, *General Economic History* (New York: Adelphi, 1927) *op. cit.*, and his *The Theory of Social and Economic Organization* (Glencoe, Ill.: Free Press, 1947).
[14] Karl Polanyi, *The Great Transformation* (Boston: Beacon, 1957).

counterpoint and further development: the age of revolutions

the production processes and eventually to the production of "factors of production." There were also various intermediate products like the "gray cloth" that putting-out merchants bought from weavers. Transportation and commercial-mediation services between spatially separated producers and consumers became necessary. Raw materials, primary production, and the land itself became increasingly involved in the market nexus.

We have a special interest in two other "factor" markets, however, those for capital and labor. The former entered a new stage of development in the Renaissance, a major symptom of which was the religious controversy over the morality of "usury." [15] Long before the industrial revolution, money lending had existed on a substantial scale organized in money markets of various sorts, some already "international." Companies in which individuals could invest free of the contingent liabilities of partnerships also existed. By the end of the seventeenth century England possessed the beginnings of a central bank, a mark of its economic advancement.

Nevertheless, the industrial revolution saw a proliferation of financial markets at a new level of organization. These developments did not culminate until the middle of the nineteenth century, however, when general incorporation acts were adopted in England and in most of the American states [16] and organized securities markets were established. One major advantage of German industry, when it surpassed British industry in the late nineteenth century, was the superior organization and spirit of enterprise of its investment banking system.[17]

Expanded financial markets provided more flexible mechanisms of adjustment for the increasingly complex and expanding economic system. More and more, money went beyond its functions as a medium of exchange and measure of value to become the primary control mechanism of the economic process. Control of money was used to influence the allocation of resources through the market mechanism. More important, the new dependence of credit creation upon large-scale financial institutions provided a type of built-in mechanism of economic growth.

The extension of the productive "chain" was of primary importance in physical production, especially in connection with the mechanisms of integration and stabilization of the economy as a whole. Increasing shares of resources were devoted to the early and intermediate stages of the progression from raw materials to consumable products.

[15] Benjamin Nelson, *The Idea of Usury: From Tribal Brotherhood to Universal Otherhood* (2nd ed.; Chicago: University of Chicago Press, 1969).

[16] For an analysis of these legal developments and their importance, see J. Willard Hurst, *Law and the Conditions of Freedom* (Madison: University of Wisconsin Press, 1956).

[17] Landes, *op. cit.*

counterpoint and further development: the age of revolutions

A particularly important trend in this connection has been the development of *generalized* physical facilities. Transportation facilities like railways would seldom be economically viable if limited to the transportation of one product. Once lines existed between given centers, however, they could be used for many purposes. Similar considerations applied to provision of mechanical power. The steam engine was one of the principal innovations of the early industrial revolution; electric power and the internal-combustion engine arrived later. Sources of energy, transmission of energy and fuel, and modes of using power were thus enhanced. Finally, the development of "tools to make tools," the machine-tool industry, also contributed to the technology of many different industries.[18]

These technological developments were closely interdependent with changes in the social organization of the productive process, especially of labor as a factor in production. The critical development was the differentiation of labor (or, more technically, of services) from the diffuse matrix in which it had been embedded. This differentiation involved distinguishing the work-role complex from the family household and also increased the "mobility of labor"—the readiness of households to respond to employment opportunities by changing residences or learning new skills. These changes affected the structures of family systems and local communities profoundly. Many features of the modern form of nuclear-family kinship structure gradually emerged during the nineteenth century. And industrial society became urbanized to a degree never before known in history.

These processes established what sociologists call the *occupational role,* specifically contingent upon status in an employing organization structurally distinct from the household.[19] Usually the employing organization has only one member in common with the household; it also has premises, disciplines, authority systems, and property distinct from those of the household. Typically the employed person receives (according to his employment status and role performance) a money income that is the main source of his household's access to the market for consumer goods. The employing organization markets its product and pays the employee wages or a salary, whereas the typical peasant or artisan sold his own products. The organization thus comes between the worker and the consumer market.

The spread of occupational roles extended the range of consumer markets because of consumers' increased dependence upon money incomes in meeting their wants. But Adam Smith's famous dictum "The division of labor depends on the extent of the market" is important in this con-

[18] *Ibid.*
[19] Neil J. Smelser, *Social Change in the Industrial Revolution* (Chicago: University of Chicago Press, 1959).

counterpoint and further development: the age of revolutions

nection: The advancing division of labor made possible increasing productivity and a rise in the standard of living among the general population.

In the factories roles were generally "occupationalized" from the bottom up. The first to become employees were propertyless wage workers, the mill hands of the textile industry. Management was generally based upon proprietorship. The owner, usually a kinship group, organized production, raised capital, set up factories, employed and supervised workers, and marketed the products. The early "capitalistic" industrial firm was thus a "two-class system," consisting of the proprietary lineage on one side and the employees on the other.[20] This system was the structural basis for the Marxist conception of "class conflict" in capitalistic society, in which ownership and organizational authority are assumed always to operate together.

Finally, we must discuss a problem that has been very much misunderstood, largely for ideological reasons. The industrial revolution emerged under a "free enterprise" system and very likely could not have *originated* under any basically different one. Furthermore, we argue that a free-enterprise economy, rather than socialism in the sense of governmental operation of the whole economy, remains the main focus of evolution. Private economic enterprise and government organization of economic matters are not, however, related in a "zero-sum" manner: An increase in one does not require a corresponding decrease in the other. As Durkheim demonstrated,[21] a highly developed free-enterprise economy, compared to a more primitive form of economic organization, requires a stronger governmental structure, not a more restricted one.

A universalistic legal system, a central feature of any industrial society, cannot exist without strong government. Furthermore, increasingly complex regulatory functions are necessary to the economy, as to other aspects of society, for example, in the control of the cyclical disturbances that upset early industrial economies.

Government and economy are interdependent. Government requires taxable resources, which are increased by increments in productivity and by the mobility of resources in a developed market system. Similarly, government, in its own participation in the labor markets, benefits from the mobility of manpower.

This interdependence involves the interchange of money and power between the market system and the system of formal organization. Not only government but also such private organizations as firms participate in the power system; conversely government participates in the market

[20] See Reinhard Bendix, *Work and Authority in Industry* (New York: Wiley, 1956).
[21] Émile Durkheim, *The Division of Labor in Society* (New York: Macmillan, 1933).

counterpoint and further development: the age of revolutions

system. The power of private units is dependent upon that of government in two critical respects beside the general institutionalization of property and contract. First, the corporation as a legal entity is at least in part a "delegation" of public authority on the basis of a publicly granted and revocable charter. The use of authority within corporate organizations is *legitimated* by this authorization.[22] Second, modern economies depend upon the credit mechanism for capitalization. Extension of credit involves the use of power by credit agencies, especially banks; they make funds available to borrowers, funds that they themselves do not "own," and bind themselves with legally enforceable contracts. This enforceability provides the basis of confidence in the time-extendability of loan relations, which partake of the inherent risk of investments that cannot "pay off" except over a considerable period.

In a modern society, underdevelopment of the power system is thus highly deleterious to the economy, and underdevelopment of the monetary and market systems is highly deleterious to the polity.

The Democratic Revolution

The democratic revolution was part of the process of differentiating the polity and the societal community. As do all processes of differentiation, it produced integration problems and, where it was successful, new mechanisms of integration.

In European societies the focal point of these problems was some degree of popular support for government in the societal community. The starting point was the conception of ordinary people as "subjects" of their monarch, with almost totally ascriptive obligations to obey his authority, which was often claimed to be divinely ordained.[23] Although the English crown's monopoly of governmental authority had fallen in the seventeenth century, as it had in a different way in Holland, even the English regime was far from "democratic"; it was rather sharply aristocratic.

Intellectual discussion during the Enlightenment made clear the internal tensions in the Continental territorial monarchies, exacerbated by the visibility of the British and Dutch examples.[24] This strain was particularly acute in France, which had gone farthest in developing the national-ethnic basis of community while at the same time retaining an old-regime absolutism. The "common" people, including some high in the bourgeoisie, were still "subjects," whereas the aristocracy, closely allied to the crown, had consolidated its privileges. These developments identi-

[22] Hurst, *op. cit.*
[23] J. W. Allen, A *History of Political Thought in the Sixtennth Century* (New York: Barnes & Noble, 1960).
[24] R. R. Palmer, *The Age of Democratic Revolution* (2 vols.; Princeton: Princeton University Press, 1959 and 1964).

counterpoint and further development: the age of revolutions

fied what "counted" in the societal community ever more closely with government, while pressing subjects not closely participating in government and its aristocratic penumbra into positions of dubious inclusion in the national community. As almost everywhere on the Continent, the central government, reinforced by the Counter-Reformation, pressed its diffuse claims to authority. The tradition of legally protected rights was much weaker on the Continent than in England.

Within the framework of a high level of national consciousness, the French Revolution demanded a community that included *all* Frenchmen and abrogated the special status of the *privilegiés*. The central concept was *citizenship*, the claim of the *whole* population to inclusion.[25]

The famous slogan of the Revolution, *Liberté, Égalité, Fraternité*, embodied the new conception of community. *Liberté* and *Égalité* symbolized the two central foci of dissatisfaction, political authoritarianism and privilege; *Fraternité* referred primarily to the broader context of belonging, "brotherhood" being a primordial symbol of community.

In the late eighteenth and nineteenth centuries the symbol of liberty had two distinct references.[26] One was paramount in England, where Adam Smith stressed economic liberty, especially in contrast with the governmental control associated with mercantilism. The other was paramount in France, where Rousseau was the most important author. It emphasized the liberty of the societal community, of the "people" vis-à-vis government. The problems of liberty of the people in this sense and liberty of the individual were not clearly distinguished, especially in the political sphere. It was the tyranny of the regime that had to be eliminated. The dictatorial tendencies of the Revolution emerged only after the power of the old regime had been at least temporarily broken.

The problem of equality is even more subtle. Whereas one can think of liberty primarily in terms of casting off restraints, equality inherently involves relations among units that are *positively* valued. Units that claim a right to equality cannot legitimately oppose recognition of the equality of others. Whereas in the context of liberty the evil is illegitimate constraint, in the context of equality it is illegitimate *discrimination*. The ideology of equality has often suggested that all differences of status or function are illegitimate, particularly if they are hierarchical. Social systems require varying kinds and degrees of social differentiation on two dimensions, however: a qualitative division of labor (in the Durkheimian sense) and a hierarchy.

The French Revolution, stressing both liberty and equality, focused

25 *Ibid.*; see also Bendix, *Nation-Building and Citizenship.*
26 See Bernard Bailyn, *The Ideological Origins of the American Revolution* (Cambridge, Mass.: Harvard University Press, 1967).

counterpoint and further development: the age of revolutions

not only upon political authority but also upon the partially distinct system of privilege for the aristocracy. Tensions had been exacerbated by the association of the *noblesse de robe* with the monarchy and the older aristocracy under the ancien régime, so that the "people" stood *against* the "privileged," who were indissolubly identified with the government. There has been enormous ideological distortion of the European aristocracies' frivolity and social irresponsibility at the expense of the people. The critical issue of "privilege" was actually the hereditary ascription of status, which conflicted with the standards of either achievement or equality or both. The Revolution raised the question of whether privilege can be a meaningful *reward* or even legitimated on instrumental grounds—unless it is demonstrated that no other way of institutionalizing responsible leadership is possible. The attack of the French Revolution on the principle of privilege was mainly led by the higher bourgeoisie, many of whose members were richer than were most aristocrats and, if not more powerful in the formal sense, perhaps more influential in governmental affairs.

In England, the aristocracy, which included the gentry, was much more "private" and less identified with the regime. In fact, reform movements were often led by members of the aristocracy; the "French" question of aristocracy versus bourgeoisie was not nearly so explicitly raised.

The Revolutionary concept of equality, in relation to differential instrumental qualifications and the hierarchical dimension of social status, emphasized *equality of opportunity*. To the extent that this emerging value pattern was institutionalized, achievement and achievement capacity became the primary criteria of eligibility for differentially valued statuses. The attainment of a status or its retention under competitive pressure could then be evaluated as a reward for significant contribution to the social system. This complex gave support to a major normative component of the industrial revolution.

The main thrust in the French Revolution, however, was against inherited aristocratic privilege and toward equality of membership status, which must be distinguished from equality of opportunity, even though the two are interdependent. The pattern of privilege under the ancien regime had divided the societal community into two primary status classes. The "common man" was a "second-class citizen," who was denied by his hereditary status access to privileges enjoyed by the aristocracy, perhaps especially tax exemptions.[27]

Marshall has analyzed equality of membership as possessing three primary components, civil, political, and social.[28] The French Revolution

[27] *Ibid.*
[28] T. H. Marshall, *Class, Citizenship, and Social Development* (Garden City, N.Y.: Anchor, 1965).

involved the first and second, whereas the third became important only in the mid-nineteenth century.

The civil component includes guarantees of what were called "natural rights"—in Locke's formulation, "life, liberty, and property." They were amplified and specified by the French Declaration of the Rights of Man and the American Bill of Rights. The revolutionary movement in France was encouraged by the fact that English and American law had already institutionalized many of these rights. The concept of "equality before the law" characterizes the civil component of equality of membership if it is taken to include both procedural and substantive protections. Here "law" means not only that enforceable through the courts but also the general patterning of the society's normative order.

The "political" component of citizenship focusses upon the democratic franchise. Although the principle of equality among citizens in the "final" voice of government dates from the ancient Greek polis, the French Revolution applied it to the government of a large-scale society and to all the people. It is impossible for modern government to give equal direct participation to all citizens. Developments have therefore been in the direction of *representative* institutions, in which political equality is focused upon the selection of top governmental leadership, generally through participation in an electoral system. The forms of these institutions vary in important ways,[29] especially between the "presidential" and "parliamentary" types and between "republics" and "constitutional" monarchies.

Despite such variation all European political systems, except the communist ones but including many such overseas societies of European origin as the United States and some members of the British Commonwealth, have evolved toward a common pattern.[30] This pattern includes two components of equality and two contextual features.

The first component of equality is universality of the franchise. The main trend has been toward universal adult suffrage; women's suffrage was adopted early in the present century in most Western nations. Only minors, aliens, and small classes of disqualified persons are now generally excluded. The other component of equality has been elimination of the *weighting* of votes. Historically, various systems have weighted votes unequally, either explicitly as in the Prussian class system of voting or implicitly as in discriminatory apportionment in the United States. The trend is, however, clearly toward the principle of one citizen, one vote, both in access to the polls and in the weight of each vote in determining electoral outcomes.

The first contextual feature is the system of formal electoral proce-

[29] See S. M. Lipset and Stein Rokkan, "Introduction," in Lipset and Rokkan, *Cleavage Structures, Party Systems, and Voter Alignment* (New York: Free Press, 1965).
[30] Stein Rokkan, "Mass Suffrage, Secret Voting, and Political Participation," in *European Journal of Sociology* (1961), 132–52.

82

dure, including rules of eligibility for voting and rules by which votes are "counted." The latter aspect is critical in establishing a *binding* relation between the individual voter's choice and the effects of many such choices on the outcome. The second contextual development is secrecy of the ballot, which further differentiates government and societal community by protecting the individual's independent participation in each. It guards the voter from pressures not only from status superiors (for example, employers) but also from status peers (for example, fellow union members).[31] This "barrier" favors political pluralization relative to the rest of the society and discourages unanimous "bloc" voting (for example, *all* trade-union members voting for socialist or other "left" parties) and encourages minorities within each interest group (or religious, ethnic, or local group) to vote differently from the majority. This structure enhances community flexibility and the possibility of both restraining and mobilizing government as an agency of change responsible to the community.

In one sense, the "social" component of citizenship is the most fundamental of the three.[32] Some form of equality of social condition as an aspect of "social justice" has been a primary theme of Western history since the French Revolution but one that did not become institutionally salient until much later. It seems that the full emergence of this theme had to await reduction in the inequalities of governmental absolutism and aristocracy, which raised new tensions between the imperatives of equality of opportunity and equality of membership. The central principle may perhaps be that members of the society must have realistic, not merely formal, opportunities to compete, with reasonable prospects of success but that the community should not accord full membership to those inherently excluded from the opportunity complex. Allowance is thus made for those, like children, who are inherently unable to compete; those, like the unskilled poor, who are severely handicapped through no fault of their own and must be "helped" to compete; and those, like the aged, who must be supported. Furthermore, there should be a "floor" under the competitive system that defines a standard of "welfare" to which all members are *entitled* as a matter of "right," not as a matter of "charity."

The third Revolutionary catchword, *Fraternité*, suggested a synthesis of the other two at a more general normative level. In a certain sense, it was the ultimate embodiment of the implications for secular Society of the Reformation. The solidary societal community that it proclaimed could not be a two-class system in any of the medieval senses—Church and state, clergy and laity, or aristocracy and commons—but had to be a *unitary* community. Its members were to be considered not only free and equal, in

[31] *Ibid.*
[32] See Marshall, *op. cit.*

counterpoint and further development: the age of revolutions

the senses that we have outlined, but also bound together in a national, autonomous solidarity. This societal community was to be differentiated from government as its superior, legitimately entitled to control it. Yet the degree of its differentiation was still far from completely modern, particularly in regard to its incomplete pluralization.

French society during the nineteenth century institutionalized the democratic pattern of societal community only partially and unstably.[33] The French Right held tenaciously to the patterns of the old régime down into the present century. It led several "experiments" in monarchical restoration and maintained a de facto ascendance in social prestige for the aristocracy and a strong, though contested, position for the established Roman Catholic Church. This conflict within France was exacerbated by the survival of the older system in most of the Continent, despite the spread of revolutionary patterns, especially through Napoleon's conquests.

Although England went much farther in the process of pluralization, a fact closely connected with its leadership in the industrial revolution, radical pressures toward democratization were absent, and the franchise was extended only gradually from 1832 on. Aristocracy remained strong in British society throughout the nineteenth century, though it was less "rigid" than in most Continental countries and less of an impediment to pluralistic differentiation and gradual democratization.[34]

The struggle over democratization was a major component of European social conflict during the nineteenth century. Napoleon was in certain respects the heir of the Revolution. The restored "legitimism" of the Holy Alliance was directed not only against French "imperialism" but also against Revolutionary ideas. Significantly, its breakdown in 1848 started in France but then became especially intense on the eastern fringe of the European system.

Through the nineteenth century, leadership of the European system remained in the northwest sector, where an increasingly sharp "dialectical" conflict emerged between the British and French attitudes. Both were essential to the emerging synthesis, the one emphasizing economic productivity and pluralization of the social structure, the other democratization of the nation-state, nationalism and a new kind of societal community.

There were also important developments in the less advanced areas, however. The emergence of imperial Germany represented a major disturbance to the European system. It fully exploited the potentials of both the industrial revolution and the undemocratic "authoritarian" state while France and Britain were still insufficiently strong and unified to cope with

[33] See Stanley Hoffmann, "Paradoxes of the French Political Community," in Hoffmann et al., In Research of France (Cambridge, Mass.: Harvard University Press, 1963).
[34] Marshall, op. cit.

84

the new power by genuinely *synthesizing* the components of modern society.

At the same time, the shadow of the "collossi" of the East and the West fell over the European system. Russia had emerged to assume a major role in the European system by contributing crucially to Napoleon's defeat and had become a primary participant in the settlement of Vienna and a guarantor of the Metternich system. By the time of World War I the United States had also emerged as unequivocally important to "the system."

the new lead society
and contemporary
modernity

six

The industrial and democratic revolutions were aspects of the great transformation by which the institutional bulwarks of the early modern system were progressively weakened. European monarchies have survived only where they have become constitutional. Aristocracy still twitches but mostly in the informal aspects of stratification systems— nowhere is it structurally central. There are still established churches, but only on the less modern peripheries like Spain and Portugal is there severe restriction on religious freedom. The broad trend is toward denominational pluralism and the separation of church asd state, though the communist countries present special problems. The industrial revolution shifted primary economic organization from agriculture and also from the commerce and handicrafts of small urban communities to extended markets.

The emergence of "full" modernity thus weakened the ascriptive framework of monarchy, aristocracy, established churches, and an economy circumscribed by kinship and localism to the point at which it no longer exercised decisive influence. Certain modern components that had already developed to some degree by the eighteenth century became increasingly important, particularly a universalistic legal system and secular culture, which had been diffused through Western society by means of the En-

86

lightenment. Further developments in the political aspects of societal community emphasized the associational principle, nationalism, citizenship, and representative government. In the economy differentiated markets developed for the factors of production, primarily labor. "Occupational" services were increasingly performed in employing organizations that were structurally differentiated from households. New patterns of effectively organizing specific functions arose, especially administration (centering in government and the military) and the new economy. The democratic revolution immensely stimulated the former, the industrial revolution the latter. Weber saw that in a later phase the two patterns tend to fuse in the bureaucratization of capitalist economy.[1] They have also, however, begun to fuse in other contexts, notably the associationalizing of the technological base of modern efficiency.

We have seen that the modern structural pattern initially crystallized in the northwest corner of Europe, whereas a secondary pattern subsequently emerged in the northeast corner, centering on Prussia. A striking parallel development occurred in the second main phase of modernization. The United States, the "first new nation," has come to play a role approximately comparable to that of England in the seventeenth century.[2] America was fertile soil for both the democratic and industrial revolutions and for combining them more intimately than had been possible in Europe. By the time of Tocqueville's visit, a synthesis of the French and English revolutions had already been achieved: The United States was as "democratic" a society as all but the extreme wing of the French Revolution had wished for, and its level of industrialization was to surpass that of England. We shall therefore concentrate in the following discussion upon the United States.

The Structure of the Societal Community

Behind the developments outlined in the preceding paragraphs were a very special religious constitution and societal community. The United States was in a position to make new departures from the principal ascriptive institutions of early modern society: monarchy, with its "subjects," rather than citizens; aristocracy; an established church; an economy committed to localism and only a little division of labor; and an ethnically defined societal community, or "nation."

American territory was initially settled mainly by one distinctive group of migrants. They were "nonconformists" in search not so much of freedom from persecution as of greater religious independence than they could en-

[1] Max Weber, *The Theory of Social and Economic Organization* (New York: Oxford University Press, 1947).
[2] Seymour M. Lipset, *The First New Nation* (New York: Basic Books, 1963).

the new lead society and contemporary modernity

joy at home.[3] They were predominantly of the Puritan persuasion, which Weber considered the core of "ascetic" Protestantism. In the colonies as a whole, however, they were divided into a number of denominations and sects.

In the early period, most notably in Congregational Massachusetts, the various colonies generally established their own churches. But a conception of the church as ideally a voluntary association emerged, in a process that passed through a decisive phase shortly before the crisis of independence,[4] though in Massachusetts full disestablishment did not occur until more than a generation later. The religious pluralism of the thirteen colonies as a whole and the rationalistic, Enlightenment-influenced cultural atmosphere set the stage for the First Amendment, which prescribed a constitutional separation of church and state for the first time since the institutionalization of Christianity in the Roman Empire.[5]

Religious pluralism rapidly spread from differences among the original colonies to pluralism within each state, in contrast to the pattern of *cuius regio, eius religio*. This pluralism formed the basis for toleration, and eventually for full inclusion, of non-Protestant elements, especially a very large Roman Catholic minority and a relatively small but important Jewish minority.[6] This inclusion has been symbolized in recent years by the election of a Roman Catholic, John F. Kennedy, to the Presidency. American society thus went beyond England and Holland in differentiating organized religion from the societal community, a process that had many important consequences. In particular, publicly sponsored and supported education as it developed in the nineteenth century was secular education. There was never, as in France, a major political struggle over that problem.

A parallel development has occurred in ethnic composition, the other principal historic basis of "nationality." The United States was for a long time an Anglo-Saxon society, which tolerated and granted legal rights to members of some other ethnic groups but did not fully include them. This problem grew acute with the arrival of waves of non-Anglo-Saxon immigrants from southern and eastern Europe, predominantly Roman Catholic and Jewish, from about 1890 to the beginning of World War I.[7] Although

[3] Perry Miller, *Errand into the Wilderness*, (New York: Harper, 1964).
[4] *Ibid.* See J. J. Loubser. "The Development of Religious Liberty in Massachusetts," unpublished doctoral dissertation, Harvard University, 1964; and Alan Heimert, *Religion and the American Mind: From the Great Awakening to the Revolution* (Cambridge, Mass.: Harvard University Press, 1966).
[5] Perry Miller, *The Life of the Mind in America: From the Revolution to the Civil War* (New York: Harcourt, 1965).
[6] Will Herberg, *Protestant, Catholic, Jew* (rev. ed.; Garden City, N.Y.: Anchor, 1960); and Talcott Parsons, "Some Comments on the Pattern of Religious Organization in the United States," in *Structure and Process in Modern Societies* (New York: Free Press, 1960).
[7] Oscar Handlin, *The Uprooted* (New York: Grosset & Dunlap, 1951).

the new lead society and contemporary modernity

the process of inclusion is still incomplete in the present century, the societal community has become ethnically pluralistic.

Negroes are still in the early stages of the inclusion process. The great bulk of the Negro population has been until recently segregated socially and geographically in the rural South, a region that has been considerably insulated from the rest of American society since the Civil War. Recently the South has been undergoing rapid "modernization" through inclusion in the society as a whole, and there has been massive migration of Negroes to the northern and western cities. These developments have stimulated a further process of inclusion that is creating acute tensions. It may, however, be predicted with considerable confidence that the long-run trend is toward successful inclusion.[8]

One reason that the American community has moved toward shedding its identity as a white, Anglo-Saxon, Protestant community is that the "WASP" formula was never by any means monolithic. Not only do the Irish speak English, but there are also many "Anglo-Saxon" Roman Catholics and many Protestant Negroes. Pluralism has also been fostered by the socialization of the newer immigrant groups in the more general societal values.

Clearly this trend offers a possibility of solution to the instability of ethnic nationalism, the problem of securing congruence between the boundaries of the societal community and the state. One particular difficulty is inherent in ethnically pluralistic systems, however. As language is a crucial focus of ethnic membership, the right of each ethnic group in a pluralistic community to use its own language can become the focus of disruptive internal tensions, as demonstrated by the conflicts between Walloons and Flemish in Belgium and English and French in Canada.[9] Where the language of one ethnic group has become the community language, great strains may be imposed upon members of other groups. There are enormous benefits in linguistic uniformity, however. Its successful adoption in a multiethnic community probably depends on two main factors. The first is the type of priority enjoyed by the ethnic group whose language becomes the national language. The second is the number of competing languages; a plurality encourages the designation of only one language as "official." In both the twentieth-century "superpowers," the societal communities have largely gone beyond simple ethnic bases and have adopted single languages.

The original settlement of American territory was by English-speaking colonists from Great Britain. Other language groups were small and

[8] Talcott Parsons, "Full Citizenship for the Negro American?" in Talcott Parsons and Kenneth Clark (eds.), *The Negro American* (Boston: Houghton-Mifflin, 1966).

[9] Hans Kohn, *The Idea of Nationalism* (New York: Macmillan, 1961).

the new lead society and contemporary modernity

geographically limited—the Dutch in New York, the French in backwoods outposts and Louisiana, the Spanish in Florida and the Southwest—and none could seriously claim to provide a second language for American society as a whole. The first large ethnically distinctive immigrant group was the Roman Catholic Irish, who spoke English (Gaelic was a romantic revival, not the actual language of Irish immigrants). As non-English-speaking Roman Catholic elements arrived, the Irish pressed for their assimilation into the English-speaking community, notably by opposing foreign-language parochial schools. Indeed, it is difficult to see how common Roman Catholic interests could have been promoted had the Roman Catholic population been split into language groups.

The Protestant immigrants (for example, the Scandinavians) were generally assimilated relatively easily, without language becoming a major issue. Jewish groups arrived in considerable numbers only quite late and did not represent any one major European language. Furthermore, they never exceeded 5 percent of the total population. The United States has thus retained English as the common language of the total societal community without a widespread feeling that it represents the "imposition" of Anglo-Saxon hegemony.

A relatively well-integrated societal community has thus been successfully established in the United States on bases that are not primarily ethnic or religious. Despite diversity within the population, it has largely escaped pressure by ethnic-linguistic or religious communities for political independence or "equal rights" in respect that would undermine the solidarity of the more inclusive community.

Important and somewhat parallel developments occurred in American patterns of ascriptive stratification, especially as compared to European patterns typified by aristocracy. The American population was overwhelmingly non-aristocratic in origin and did not develop an indigenous aristocracy.[10] Furthermore, a considerable proportion of the originally upper-class elements left the country during the American Revolution. Granting of titles came to be forbidden by the Constitution, and factors like landed proprietorship and wealth have no legal recognition as criteria for government office and authority. Although American society has always been differentiated internally by class, it has never suffered the aftermath of aristocracy and serfdom that persisted so long in Europe; the nearest approximation appeared in the South. The participation of the wealthier and more educated groups in government has been disproportionate, but there has also been a persistent populist strain and relative political mobility, advancement coming first through wealth and more recently through education.

[10] Clinton Rossiter, *Seedtime of the Republic* (New York: Harcourt, 1953).

the new lead society and contemporary modernity

American society thus abandoned the tradition of aristocracy with only a mild revolutionary disturbance. It also lacked the heritage of Europe's peasant classes. As an industrial working class developed, the typical European level of "class consciousness" never emerged, largely because of the absence of aristocratic and peasant elements.[11]

The American system has also carried differentiation between government and societal community very far. For government and societal community to become highly differentiated, the right to hold office must be dissociated from ascription, from attachment to monarchy and aristocracy, and associated with achievement. Furthermore, authority must be limited to the legally defined powers of office, so that private prerogatives, property interests, and the like are strictly separated from those of office. Finally, the elective principle requires that holding office be contingent upon constituent support; loss of office through electoral defeat is an inherent risk. The independence of the legal system from the executive and legislative branches of government has been one primary mechanism for generating and maintaining this kind of differentiation.

Another mechanism has expressed the connection between the government and community stratification. The newly independent nation opted for a republican form of government (with elaborate precautions against absolutism) [12] linked with the societal community through the franchise. Although the franchise was originally restricted, especially by property qualifications, it was extended rapidly, and universal manhood suffrage, except for Negroes, was attained relatively early in the nineteenth century. The highest government authority was universally vested in elected officials: the President and members of the Congress, the state governors and members of state legislatures. The sole exception has been the appointment of Federal (and increasingly state) judges, with the expectation or formal requirement that they be professional lawyers.

A distinctive competitive party system based upon the engagement in politics of broad segments of the societal community soon emerged.[13] It has been relatively fluid, oriented toward a pluralistic structure of "interest groups," rather than toward the regional, religious, ethnic, or class solidarities more typical of Europe.

The societal community must be articulated not only with the religious and political systems but also with the economy. In the United States the factors of production, including land and labor, have been rela-

---

[11] Louis Hartz, The Liberal Tradition in America (New York: Harcourt, 1955).
[12] Rossiter, op. cit.; and Merrill Jensen, The Articles of Confederation (Madison: University of Wisconsin Press, 1940).
[13] William N. Chambers, Political Parties in a New Nation, 1776–1809 (New York: Oxford University Press, 1963); and Richard P. McCormick, The Second American Party System (Chapel Hill: University of North Carolina Press, 1966).

the new lead society and contemporary modernity

tively free of ascriptive ties, and the Federal Constitution has guaranteed their free movement among the different states. This freedom has encouraged a high degree of division of labor and the development of an extensive market system. Locally oriented and traditionally directed economic activities and the ascriptive community structures in which they were embedded have thus been undermined, which has had important consequences for the stratification system; to the extent that the latter was rooted in occupational structure, it was pushed toward universalism and an open class structure but not toward radical egalitarianism.

The American societal community that emerged from these developments was primarily *associational*. This characteristic was rooted in certain components of the value system. Universalism, which had its "purest" early modern expression in the ethics of ascetic Protestantism, has exerted strong and continuing "value pressure" toward inclusion—now reaching to the whole of the Judeo-Christian religious community and beginning to extend beyond it. Of course, the inclusion component alone could lead to a static, universalistic tolerance. It is, however, complemented by an activist commitment to building a good society in accordance with Divine Will that underlies the drive toward mastery of the various social environments through expansion in territory, economic productivity, knowledge, and so on. The *combination* of these two components has much to do with the associational emphasis in modern social structure—political and "social" democracy being conspicuous aspects.

The associational emphasis has been enhanced in the United States by the increasing elimination of ethnic membership and social class as ascriptively constitutive structures. In the early modern phase the most important basis of community in Europe was ethnic-national. Yet the coincidence between ethnic membership and territorial organization throughout most of Europe was incomplete. Ethnic-centered "nationalism" was thus not an adequate substitute for religion as a basis of societal solidarity, even as it gained in importance with "secularization" and the inclusion of religious diversity within the same political jurisdiction.

The most important new basis of inclusion in the societal community has been *citizenship*, developing in close association with the democratic revolution.[14] Citizenship can be dissociated from ethnic membership, with its strong tendency toward nationalism and even "racism," which provides a sharp ascriptive criterion of belonging. The alternative has been to define belonging in universalistic terms, which inevitably must include reference to voluntary "allegiance," although probably no societal community can

[14] T. H. Marshall, *Class, Citizenship and Social Development* (Garden City, N.Y.: Anchor, 1965).

the new lead society and contemporary modernity

be a purely voluntary association.[15] The institutionalization of access to citizenship through *naturalization*, regardless of the ethnic origins of individuals, represents an important break with the imperative of ethnic membership.

The development of the American pattern of citizenship has broadly followed that outlined by Marshall for Great Britain, starting with the "civic" component, as he calls it, and developing the political and social components from there. The social component, though it has lagged behind that of the principal European societies, has been greatly extended through public education, social security, welfare policies, insurance, union benefits, and other means in the present century. Contemporary concern with problems of poverty marks a new phase in that development. On the whole, the structural outline of "citizenship" in the new societal community is complete, though not yet fully institutionalized. There are two mutually elated stress points, the present salience of which is an index of the importance of the new structures: race and poverty. They involve above all the need to extend the processes of inclusion and upgrading still farther.

A highly developed legal system is central to a stable societal community that has dispensed with religious and ethnic uniformity as radically as has American society. The Puritan tradition and the Enlightenment fostered a strong predilection for a written Constitution, with its echoes of covenant and social contract.[16] An individualistic fear of authoritarianism had much to do with the separation of government powers.[17] A federal structure was practically necessitated by the legal separation of the colonies. All three circumstances placed a premium on legal forms and on agencies charged with legal functions. Also many of the framers of the Constitution had legal training. Even though they provided for only one Supreme Court, without specifying membership qualifications and with very little specification of its powers, they did lay the foundations for an especially strong emphasis on the legal order.

But three important developments were not clearly foreseen by the Founding Fathers. First was the importance of judicial review in settling conflicts among the branches of Federal government, among the states, and between the states and the Federal government. The second was the adoption and further development of English common law and the resulting proliferation of "judge-made" law. Finally, there was the expansion and

[15] See Karl W. Deutsch, *Nationalism and Social Communication* (Cambridge, Mass.: M.I.T. Press, 1953).

[16] See Edward S. Corwin, The *"Higher Law"*: *Background of American Constitutional Law* (Ithaca, N.Y.: Cornell University Press, 1955).

[17] Bernard Bailyn, "General Introduction," in *Pamphlets of the American Revolution* (Cambridge, Mass.: Harvard University Press, 1965).

professionalization of legal practice. In contrast to the system in Continental Europe, the legal profession, though participating freely in politics, has not been organized about governmental functions.[18]

Because the separation of powers and Federalism have decentralized American government to such an extent, legal institutions have been particularly important in the continuous attenuation of local autonomy, so critical a force in all early modern societies. The recent reintegration of the South into the nation is the most conspicuous example.

The Constitutional framework strongly emphasizes universalistic criteria of citizenship. These criteria have undergone fairly continuous evolution, involving both specification and generalization, in crucial interdependence with the evolution of the legal system, particularly the interpretive contributions of the Federal judiciary. One consequence has been pressure toward inclusion, most dramatically of Negroes.

At a more general level there is an important duality in what Marshall calls the "civic" component of citizenship, which has become particularly prominent in the United States because of this nation's special reliance on a written Constitution. One aspect is the more familiar citizen's rights and obligations as they have been formulated in the course of legal history. This component, of course, covers a very wide range, and certain principles of "equality before the law" are prominent almost throughout. Back of it, however, stand more general principles, first embodied in the Bill of Rights and extended both by amendment and by judicial interpretation, a particularly important phase of which has occurred recently. There is in this complex a strong egalitarian emphasis, increasingly stressed over time, on the basic equalities of citizens' rights to protection, certain freedoms, certain basic conditions of welfare, and opportunities, especially perhaps access to education and occupational development. In fact, it seems correct to say that, at least in principle, the new societal community has come to be defined as a company of equals. Departures from the egalitarian principle must be justified, either on the basis of incapacity to participate fully—as among small children—or of being qualified for special contributions, as through competence, to the societal welfare.

The Educational Revolution and
the Contemporary Phase of Modernization

The recent educational revolution is as important as the industrial and democratic revolutions have been. As a "child" of the Enlightenment, education has consisted primarily of inculcating intellec-

[18] See Roscoe Pound, *The Spirit of the Common Law* (Boston: Beacon, 1963); and James Willard Hurst, *Law and the Conditions of Freedom* (Madison: University of Wisconsin Press, 1956).

the new lead society and contemporary modernity

tual disciplines grounded in secular philosophy and organized in the natural sciences, the humanities, and the social sciences. These secular disciplines have become institutionalized in the "academic" system, that is, the system of higher education based on the universities. The universities are centers not only of instruction but also of the systematic pursuit of new knowledge through research. Compared to its medieval and early modern antecedents, the contemporary university has an altogether new comprehensiveness.[19]

One aspect of this new revolution is the spread of basic education. Before the early nineteenth century even elementary literacy had not extended beyond a small élite in any large-scale society. To attempt to educate the *whole* population was a radical departure. Formal education has had a long history, but until the educational revolution it was limited to a small proportion of any generation and generally of much shorter duration than it is today. This movement has thus meant an immense extension of equality of opportunity. A decreasing proportion of each successive generation has been handicapped by lack of access to educational qualifications for various statuses, both occupational roles and life styles. The spread of coeducation has been a particularly conspicuous egalitarian development.

At the same time, however, the educational system is necessarily selective. Differences in inborn ability to do intellectual work and in family orientations and individual motivations mean that levels of educational attainment and distinction vary. This factor has become prominent in what some currently call the "meritocracy," which, however compatible with ideals of equality of opportunity, does introduce new forms of substantive inequality into the modern social system.

A main feature of the educational revolution has been continuous extension of the education of the population beyond basic literacy. A major step has been the expansion of secondary education to the point at which the high-school "dropout" is viewed as a problem, lacking certain status characteristics of full membership in the societal community. Furthermore, rapidly increasing numbers of people are involved in higher education. The relatively stable situation of late nineteenth-century Europe accorded higher education to a small élite group, never more than 5 percent of the age group. The United States has broken decisively with this limitation; the proportion of youth receiving some higher education is around 40 percent and is steadily edging upward.

The creative-innovative aspect of the educational system has greatly increased its momentum. The earlier "inventions" of the industrial revo-

[19] Joseph Ben-David, *The Sociology of Science* (Englewood Cliffs, N.J.: Prentice-Hall, 1971); and Talcott Parsons and Gerald M. Platt, "Some Considerations on the American Academic Profession," *Minerva*, 6, No. 4 (Summer 1968), pp. 497–523.

lution were overwhelmingly the work of "practical men." Applied science did not begin to have a serious impact upon technology until the late nineteenth century. But technology has now become highly dependent upon research "payoffs," involving ever-wider ranges of the natural sciences, from nuclear physics to genetics, and also the social or "behavioral" sciences, perhaps most obviously economics and some branches of psychology. The social sciences share with the natural sciences the benefits of some striking innovations in the technology of research. For example, mathematical statistics and computer technology facilitate the objective investigation of large populations and extend the range of empirical procedures.[20]

The emphasis in the United States on an *associational* pattern of social development favored early initiation of the educational revolution and its extension farther than has occurred in any other society. This revolution in turn strengthened the associational trend, primarily through its effects upon the stratification and occupational systems. Certain ascriptive elements in the system of stratification have been generally eroded.

Of course, the hereditary principle has given way only slowly and not yet completely. As long as kinship and family remain important, it probably cannot be altogether eliminated. Family solidarity requires that children share the advantages and disadvantages of their parents during their earlier years, and the premium on competence in the larger world is so high that pressures to perpetuate approximate status from generation to generation are unavoidable.[21] But this requirement is very different from hereditary privilege as such.

The twentieth century opened a new phase in the transition from hereditary ascriptive and totally nonascriptive stratification. Each of the first two revolutions had generated an ideology embodying the aspirations to nonascriptive status of certain groups. In the industrial revolution the ideology extolled "pursuit of self-interest" by the individual for his own (and implicitly his family's) economic advancement. The ideal participant in this competitive system was the "self-made man," who linked his inborn capacity to the opportunities opened up by a competive market system: Allegedly the most capable succeeded most fully. Associated with the democratic revolution was the ideology of political equality among citizens, in contrast to the ascriptive inequalities of the system of "privilege," aristocracy, and governmental absolutism.

The ideological dilemma of capitalism versus socialism was deeply

20 See Harvey Brooks, "Scientific Concepts and Cultural Change," in Gerald Holton (ed.), *Science and Culture* (Boston: Beacon, 1966).
21 Talcott Parsons, "A Revised Analytical Approach to the Theory of Social Stratification," in Talcott Parsons, *Essays in Sociological Theory* (New York: Free Press, 1954).

96

grounded in this pair of conceptions, neither of which considered the aristocratic system acceptable. The capitalist alternative emphasized, first, freedom from the ascriptive past, then protection from governmental "interference." The socialist alternative proposed the mobilization of governmental power to institute fundamental equality, ignoring almost completely the exigencies of economic efficiency (though the emphases on development and defense have been very strong in the Soviet Union) and governmental effectiveness in other connections. Both failed to ground themselves in adequate conceptions of the societal community and of the conditions necessary to maintain its solidarity.[22]

The focus of the new phase is the educational revolution, which in a certain sense synthesizes the themes of the industrial and democratic revolutions: equality of opportunity and equality of citizenship. The "native ability" of the individual to attain a *just* standing directly through market competition is no longer assumed. Instead, stratification by ability is recognized as mediated through a complex series of stages in the socialization process. Increasingly, there are opportunities for the relatively disadvantaged to succeed through selection, regulated to an unusual degree by universalist norms.

The "utopianism" of complete political equality is modified by structures intermediate between the "absolute" individual and the ultimate national collectivity. These structures do not preclude inequalities as such and even legitimate some forms of it—but they tend to minimize both the ascriptive fixity of such inequalities and the arbitrariness of their imposition. People are both "trained" and selected according to *socialized* capacity for the more responsible roles, which require higher levels of competence and carry higher levels of reward, including income, political influence, and to a lesser extent power.

Education is a particularly important factor in the general stratification system, in socialist as well as in free-enterprise societies of the modern system.[23] Future changes will have to build on this pattern, rather than bypassing it. They cannot be based upon relatively "pure" economic criteria of selection, the enforcement of "flat" equality by political authority, or the presumption that such equality will arise "spontaneously" if only certain barriers are removed, which is essentially the eighteenth-century romantic conception of the goodness of "natural man."

The educational revolution is having a profound and growing impact on the occupational structure of society, especially in the direction of general upgrading. The increasing importance of the "professions" is especially significant. Sociological discussion has tended to consider occupational

[22] See Marshall, *op. cit.*
[23] See R. Bendix and S. M. Lipset, *Class, Status, and Power* (2nd ed., New York: Free Press, 1965).

97

roles as part of the pattern of "bureaucracy," which stresses hierarchical organization and "line" authority. The professional component, however, is most effectively institutionalized in another pattern, the "collegial," a form of *association* in which membership involves an occupational role, a "job," not casual participation.[24]

The professional complex reaches back into classical antiquity and the Middle Ages, especially including the priesthood and the practice of law and medicine. The new phase began with emphasis on scientific competence, first in law and in the "scientific medicine" of the later nineteenth century and then in many branches of engineering and other applied sciences, as well as in the social-behavioral fields.

The competence required in the professions is generally attainable only through advanced formal training, which now occurs in academic settings. The modern university has thus become the keystone in the professional arch. The profession par excellence is the academic, the profession of seeking and transmitting knowledge. It is surrounded by a ring of professions charged with applying knowledge to social order (law), health (medicine), effectiveness in governmental and private collectivities (administration), efficient use of the nonsocial environment (technology), and so on.[25]

The educational revolution, through the development of the academic complex and channels for applying academic competence, has thus begun to transform the whole structure of modern society. Above all, it reduces the relative importance of two major ideological concerns, the market and bureaucratic organization. The emerging emphasis is on associational organization, especially its collegial form.

Pattern Maintenance and Societal Community

Pattern maintenance is, we have argued, one of the four basic functional requirements of any society (or other action system). We define it, first, as the maintenance of the basic pattern of values institutionalized in the society and, second, as the shaping and maintenance of the appropriate motivational commitments of individuals in the society. The religious and educational developments that we have traced represent a major change in the American pattern-maintenance system.

The pluralization of the American religious complex, culminating in the inclusion of large non-Protestant groups, has, in one sense, been a process of "secularization," especially in contrast to the functioning of the older established church. As the values of society are rooted in religion,

---

[24] See Talcott Parsons, "Professions," in *International Encyclopedia of the Social Sciences* (New York: Macmillan, 1968).
[25] *Ibid.*

the new lead society and contemporary modernity

one possible consequence of the pluralization of religion is the destruction of the moral or value consensus. This destruction has, however, by and large not occurred in the United States. Value *generalization* has been much more important: The underlying moral consensus has persisted, but it is now defined at a higher level of generality than in the European societies that have institutionalized internal religious uniformity. These highly general values are, through specification, made applicable to the numerous structural contexts necessary in modern societies. We thus insist that American society and, in somewhat different ways, other modern societies maintain strong moral commitments that have survived through, and have even been strengthened by, religious pluralism and secularization.

Contemporary social structure is characterized by a special kind of integration with the cultural system. In a sense modernity began with the secularization of the medieval integration of society and religion, resulting in both the Renaissance and the Reformation. The societal *system* has since undergone a series of "declarations of independence" from close cultural— especially religious—"supervision." This independence has successively involved three main foci: legal order, first institutionalized in seventeenth-century England; national-political order, especially in pre-Revolutionary France; and market-economic order, especially in the aftermath of the industrial revolution.

The newest phase returns to primary concern with cultural elements. The focus is not religion, however, but the secular "intellectual disciplines" and perhaps, in a special sense, the "arts," whether or not they are defined as "fine." Whereas philosophy was in the ascendance in the early modern phase, "science" has become so in the twentieth century, above all through extending its scope to the social and behavioral fields and even to the humanities. The educational revolution has introduced mechanisms by which the new cultural standards, especially those embodied in the intellectual disciplines, are institutionalized in ways that partly replace traditional religion.

This new pattern is not without its strains. Unlike a century ago, when the religious implications of Darwinism stimulated bitter controversies, there has been relatively little recent ideological agitation about science. There has been much concern with "culture," however, especially the arts and some aspects of philosophy, one theme being an "aristocratic" disdain of "mass culture" expressed by such figures as T. S. Eliot, Dwight MacDonald, and Ortega y Gasset. Even concern within the religious context has a different flavor from that of the nineteenth-century conflict with science. One aspect of this concern is ecumenism, so widely heralded by "liberals," especially the Roman Catholic shift since the papacy of John XXIII and Vatican II. Another is the new skepticism about all traditional and organized religion, as in the atheist branch of existentialism

(Sartre) [26] and the "God is dead" movement within Protestantism.

Intellectual alienation seems to be primarily a manifestation of strains involved in "value generalization." The value specificity of certain older symbolic systems has hindered the establishment of a *moral* consensus that, at the level of total societal values, could have more integrative than divisive effects. We call resistance to value generalization "fundamentalism." It has been conspicuous in religious contexts, often closely linked with extreme societal conservatism, as among the Dutch Calvinists in South Africa. Indeed, the Fascist movements of the twentieth century have on the whole been fundamentalist in this sense. We can also speak of a fundamentalism of the extreme left, from certain phases of the Communist Party to the current New Left.

There have also been major changes in the mechanisms by which appropriate motivational patterns are created and sustained among members of the society, which is the second focus of the pattern-maintenance function. Some of these changes have involved the family.[27] The differentiation between employing organizations and households has removed most economically productive activity from the home. For a variety of reasons this shift has created strong pressures toward isolating the nuclear family: the married couple and its dependent children. The breadwinner of the household—usually the adult male—is involved in an occupational world in which he is evaluated primarily by performance. This evaluation is incompatible with a status system that emphasizes ascribed positions, for either individuals or households, in a tight kinship or ethnic system.

Isolation does not imply the radical breaking of ties to extended kin, especially members of the spouses' families of orientation, which typically remain important. The nuclear family has, however, become increasingly independent with respect to property, community status, and even religious and ethnic commitment. A critical index of this independence is the decline of arranged marriages, which contrasts with the emphasis on the solidarity of lineages in both peasant and aristocratic statuses.

The dependence of the family, both in status and in income terms, on occupational earnings places a premium on residential mobility. The favored residence is for a single family, rented or purchased. Geographic mobility has tended to weaken not only kinship ties but also certain general community ties of a *Gemeinschaft* character. In fact, there are strong emphases on privacy, and little presumption of intimacy with one's neighbors.

These developments enhance the significance of the family as pro-

---

26 See Michel Crozier, "The Cultural Revolution: Notes on the Changes in the Intellectual Climate in France," in Stephen R. Graubard (ed.), A *New Europe?* (Boston: Beacon, 1966).

27 Talcott Parsons, "The Kinship System of the Contemporary United States," in *Essays in Sociological Theory* (New York: Free Press, 1954).

the new lead society and contemporary modernity

vider of a secure emotional base for its members' participation in society. Not only have other diffuse emotional relationships been undermined, but also in certain respects family members are under increasing stress outside the home because of obligations placed upon them at work and school. The general process has thus been one of differentiation, the nuclear family focusing on pattern maintenance connected with its members' personalities to the exclusion of other functions.

These developments have placed considerable strain upon the house-wife, who must be increasingly self-reliant in fulfilling her obligations to her husband and children. Furthermore, the woman's role has expanded in important ways, as symbolized by women's suffrage and participation in education and the labor force.

The educational revolution has had important consequences in this context also. Increasingly, socialization with respect to achievement in nonfamilial roles is left to educational institutions, which are differentiated from the family. It is the educational system and not the family that increasingly serves as the direct source of labor for the economy. Similarly, it is the educational system, and not kinship, that increasingly determines the distribution of individuals within the stratification system.

We can at this point venture a more general interpretation of the educational revolution than has so far been advanced. Two revolutions shaped early modernity: the industrial, which differentiated the economy and the polity from each other and developed new links between them, and the democratic, which involved analogous changes between the polity and the societal community. We suggest that the educational revolution is the climax of similar changes between the societal community and the pattern-maintenance system—and through it the cultural system. We have traced the differentiation of the societal community and the pattern-maintenance system through many steps, especially the development of a normative order and the definition of a societal community not grounded directly in religion. The educational revolution is a further step in this secularization. It also, however, involves important integrative mechanisms, among them a means for institutionalizing secular culture. Furthermore, it reflects an increasing emphasis upon socialized capacity as a criterion of full membership in the societal community, as well as of distributing new members through the stratification system.[27]

Polity and Societal Community

The differentiation between societal community and the political system is most fundamental to government but could

[27] Talcott Parsons and Gerald M. Platt, "Higher Education, Changing Socialization, and Contemporary Student Dissent," in Matilda Riley, et al. (eds.), Aging and Society (New York: Russell Sage, 1971).

be viewed in the broader analytical setting of the "political factor" of collective goal attainment, regardless of the status of the referent collectivity.[28]

The most important development is the focusing of political function in the specific role type that we call office, elective and appointive, which is broadly correlated with two types of collectivities, the associational and the bureaucratic, and in the institution of citizenship. When elective office is a complement of citizenship, government is differentiated from the societal community, and the members of that community (and for the most part its territorial subdivisions) become *constituents* of it. Through the franchise they are the ultimate source of its formal power—within a constitutional framework—and the ultimate beneficiaries, individually, in groups, and as a community, of government contributions to societal functioning.[29] Elective office, with power to make and implement collectively binding decisions, is thus at the heart of the leadership function. In large-scale societies the mobilization of support, both for election and for decision making, tends to be achieved through political parties that mediate between the government leadership and the numerous "interest groups" in the constituency.[30]

As elective office is not usually a permanent job, it seldom approaches an "occupational" role type. Stable democracies, however, generally have a class of relatively "professional" politicians whose primary concern is to occupy elective office or to assist those aspiring to it, party organizers, for example. In the United States federalism and the decentralization of local governmental units have enlarged this class.[31] Anchorage in appointive office and in private sector (for example, in legal practice), in order to obtain occupational security and personal property, are, however, essential to those who commit themselves to political leadership. In general, democracies urgently need a functional equivalent to aristocracy as the security base for leadership.

In line with the size and complexity of the society, an extensive system of governmental administrative agencies has developed but without upsetting a certain balance between the "political" (elective) and the bureaucratic components of government.

---

[28] See Talcott Parsons, "The Political Aspect of Social Structure and Process," in David Easton (ed.), *Varieties of Political Theory* (Englewood Cliffs, N.J.: Prentice-Hall, 1966), reprinted in Talcott Parsons, *Politics and Social Structure* (New York: Free Press, 1969). Several other essays in the latter volume are also relevant.
[29] *Ibid.*
[30] Talcott Parsons, " 'Voting' and the Equilibrium of the American Political System" and "On the Concept of Political Power," in Parsons, *Politics and Social Structure* (New York: Free Press, 1969), and of course an immense literature.
[31] See V. O. Key, *Politics, Parties, and Pressure Groups* (5th ed.; New York: Crowell, 1964).

the new lead society and contemporary modernity

What is true of the democratic polity as an associational collectivity is, with appropriate adaptations, broadly true as well of the other associations that have proliferated in modern societies. The problems of associations vary according to size, complexity, interest, and internal conflicts. The problem of securing a sufficiently independent position for leadership, *across* these partisan divisions, is, however, always crucial.

The choice between centralization, which enhances collective effectiveness, and decentralization, which permits "representativeness," freedom of expression, and the pursuits of interest by groups, is a general dilemma for democratic associations.[32] Connected with this dilemma is the matter of incentives to become integrated with the collective enterprise, as opposed to "going it alone." Broadly speaking, the institutionalization of associational patterns is correlated with intracommunity pluralization. When a collectivity has associative functions but the exercise of authority is sharply dictatorial, we may assume strong obstacles to full institutionalization. Another index of incomplete institutionalization is the insistence by individuals and groups on recognition of their particular and partial "rights" by means of techniques ranging from simple assertion through organized protest to obstruction. Indeed, when basic interests are at stake, the optimal functioning of complex democratic associations involves a delicate balancing of many factors.

Although representative democracy has proved to be a relatively workable solution at the government level under some circumstances and in some private associations, it evidently cannot be extended to all organizational contexts. In representative democracy the elected component can be linked to bureaucratic organization as the "nonbureaucratic top," the importance of which Weber emphasized.[33] Another important device for filling this role is the fiduciary board, which is not only prominent in nonprofit sectors but is also becoming in fact the main governing agency of the large private business corporation.

Bureaucratic organization is characterized by predominantly appointive office, emphasis on effective collective goal attainment, use of authority to coordinate implementation of centrally adopted plans, and a strong hierarchical structure. Criteria connected with elective office, like subordination to universalist norms and the separation of the private and official spheres, apply there as well, however.[34] The spread of bureaucracy, both public and private, has been a hallmark of later modernization. In nineteenth-century Europe, civil service expanded but had difficulty in

[32] See S. M. Lipset and Stein Rokkan (eds.), *Party Systems and Voter Alignments* (New York: Free Press, 1967), especially the Introduction.
[33] See Max Weber, *Theory of Social and Economic Organization* (Glencoe, Ill.: Free Press, 1947), pp. 324 ff.
[34] Weber, *The Theory of Social and Economic Organization.*

remaining independent of aristocratic connections, as in France, in England, and somewhat less in Prussia. In the United States this tendency was strongly counteracted by the "spoils system" and democratic populism.[35]

Bureaucratic elements probably began to emerge close to, though not quite at, the top of government. In industry, however, they emerged at the bottom, with the employment of "laborers," whereas what we now call "managerial" and "technical" functions along with ownership, were mainly in the hands of an ascriptive proprietary element. This situation has changed, especially through the separation of ownership from "control," or active management, in the large corporation during the last half-century.[36] Although owners still exercise some authority in a fiduciary sense, for example, in the selection of managers and in setting broad policy, management is organized predominantly in occupational roles, which depend little or not at all upon personal property rights or lineage structures in which property rights are institutionalized. Recently higher management has become increasingly "professionalized" as technical qualifications and formal training increase in importance. Competence is no longer primarily a matter of "horse sense" and a diploma from the "school of hard knocks."

The combination of the spreading democratic revolution and the differentiation of modern societies has, as in other contexts, been a primary source of both new freedoms and adaptive capacities, on one hand, and of new integrative strains, on the other. The new phase that is the subject of this chapter has involved, in the United States and in most modern societies, the completion of the universalization of the franchise within the particular constituency. There has also been a notable spread of this pattern of equal membership and power within a wide range of private associations, though just what the limits of this process will turn out to be, for example, in such organizations as universities, remains to be seen.

At the same time, the increase in the scale and the burden of collective responsibility of associational systems has intensified the need for effective and responsible leadership, which presumably cannot be provided without considerable concentration of power. On course, administrative bureaucracy is one fundamental way of meeting this need, but the problem of accountability within such organizations is acute, and the modern solution has been to make bureaucracy ultimately responsible to electorates but more immediately to elective officers of the political system: in the

---

[35] The classic discussion is M. Ostrogorski, *Democracy and the Party System in the United States* (New York: Macmillan, 1912).

[36] A. A. Berle and Gardiner C. Means, *The Modern Corporation and Private Property* (New York: Commerce Clearing House, 1952).

104

American government in particular, the executive and legislative branches. This solution clearly involves giving immense power to elected officials— presidents and governors of states, as well as members of Congress and of state legislatures. They in turn are held accountable through the electoral process, which may, from the present point of view, be regarded as a device for handling the inevitable tension between the egalitarian basis of citizens' rights and participation, on one hand, and the sheer functional exigencies of effective collective action, on the other.

The professions have also been increasingly involved in business, other areas of the "private sector," and government. Professional competence is not usually organized in "line authority" patterns, even in a "rational-legal" framework. This difference has modified both public and private "bureaucratic" organizations, reducing the importance of line authority, so that the organizations have become more associational, for it is essential to secure the cooperation of specialists without asserting sheer authority.[37] Much of modern "bureaucracy" thus verges on the "collegial" pattern.[38] This "collegial" pattern, modifiing bureaucracy in an associational direction, involves membership roles that are occupational; participation is a "full-time job." Collegial responsibilities cannot be specified in the fashion that line authority ordains for primarily bureaucratic organizations. Nor are they peripheral and segmental as are membership responsibilities in associations more generally, including the political component of citizenship; a "full-time voter" would be highly peculiar in a pluralistic polity, though some such concept perhaps describes the Communist Party member.

The collegial pattern is today perhaps most fully institutionalized in the academic world, which, contrary to what many have argued, is not giving way to bureaucratization,[39] even though higher education has recently undergone unprecedented expansion. The basic equality of "colleagues" in a faculty or department is in particularly sharp and persistent contrast with bureaucratic hierarchy. A second distinctive feature of collegial structure is election, as distinguished from appointment from above. Most modern academic "appointment" systems involve a complex balance: Fiduciary agencies (for example, boards of trustees) usually have "final" authority, whereas professional peers have control at important stages in selections. The imposition of an appointee explicitly unacceptable to his prospective colleagues is virtually nonexistent in the higher-level academic

[37] Parsons, *Structure and Process in Modern Societies,* Chapters 1, 2.
[38] It is notable that the issue of "collegiality," as distinct from papal monarchy has recently become prominent in the Roman Catholic Church, under the stimulus Vatican II.
[39] Parsons and Platt, *op. cit.*

the new lead society and contemporary modernity

institutions. Professors elect their colleagues, at least indirectly, if not directly.[40]

Many organizations stereotyped as bureaucracies have become "collegialized" in many ways. Modern government is not predominantly bureaucratic, not only because it has been "democratized" through elective office and responsiveness to the public but also because its internal structure, especially its "executive branch," is collegialized to a considerable degree. Furthermore, the progressive attenuation of owners' control of economic organizations has not resulted only in bureacratization, though the latter has been widespread in large-scale organizations. With the increasing importance of scientific technology, academically trained professionals have become ever more necessary in industry, not only because of their substantive contributions but also because of their impact on organizational structure. The most recent phase has brought large-scale industrial employment of research scientists, as well as engineers, with corresponding developments in fields like health and educational services.

Economy and Societal Community

As it has evolved into the contemporary phase, the economy has departed considerably from the classical pattern delineated in nineteenth-century "capitalist" ideology. It is subject not only to *institutional* control, especially legal regulation based on laws of contract and property, but also to a complex system of constraints and regulations through government price-policies, oligopolistic business practices, and collective bargaining, to name a few. There is also substantial redistribution of resources, particularly through the use of tax revenues to subsidize many groups and activities beyond the primary functions of government, ranging from relief of the indigent to subsidies for scientific research.

Nevertheless, the market system is still an autonomous and differentiated subsystem of American society.[41] The rigid opposition between a "free enterprise" system, with minimal social and governmental controls, and "socialism," with government ownership and control of *all* the principal means of production, has proved to be unrealistic. The emerging pattern corresponds to a general modern trend toward structural differentiation and pluralization. In societies broadly identified as having "free

---

[40] For some purposes a third process of achieving occupational membership must be considered: "hiring." It suggests the naked economic nexus, treatment of the incumbent's service as a "commodity." Modern occupational systems, partly influenced by union organization, have clearly been developing away from such economic casualness for all but a decreasing minority.

[41] Talcott Parsons and Neil J. Smelser, *Economy and Society* (New York: Free Press, 1956).

106

the new lead society and contemporary modernity

enterprise" economies, only the rear guard of the political Right that opposes all modification of ninteenth-century laissez-faire would seriously challenge this judgment. Indeed, the instability inherent in even approximations of the "pure" capitalist system, as formulated by both its proponents and its socialist opponents, is a cogent reason for treating the nineteenth-century phase of modern society as transitional.

Around the turn of the century the United States surpassed England and then Germany in quantitative economic growth. This rapid development resulted from a variety of conditions. At Independence, the United States had fewer than 4 million people, concentrated along the Atlantic coast but with room for relatively unhindered westward expansion. Partly because of British control of the seas, the "imperialist" energies of France and Spain soon ebbed in the Americas. It was therefore possible for the United States peacefully to purchase Florida and the Louisiana Territory; somewhat later Mexico put up only weak resistance to further territorial expansion, which made room for population growth and provided immense economic resources of all sorts. Such expansion also predisposed the nation to a liberal immigration policy, which, among its many important consequences, guaranteed much of the labor force for industrialization.

The development of monetary, banking, and credit institutions grounded in "commercial banking" was rapid and extensive, though these instruments were very unstable throughout the nineteenth century. Thanks to the banking system, the circulating medium consists mainly of bank deposits—cash represents a small fraction—and supports many forms of credit, corporate securities, and even the public debt.[42] The credit system favors continuing economic innovation as the contemporary academic system favors "cognitive innovation." No other society rivals the United States in "monetarization" of economic affairs, especially the use of banks and credit instruments.

The American pattern of capitalism has been particularly distinctive in two respects. The first was the development of mass production, pioneered by the Ford Motor Company. Because mass production is necessarily oriented toward large consumer markets, mostly domestic, it came to be understood that profits depend not only upon the "share of the market" captured by a particular firm but also upon the total disposable income of the consumers. Henry Ford's high-wage policy, instituted quite apart from labor-union pressure, marked a turn toward production that was capital-intensive, rather than labor-intensive. This shift has resulted in a continuing relative decline in the *manufacturing* labor force, despite immense increases in production. There have been corresponding

---

[42] J. M. Keynes, *The General Theory of Employment, Interest, and Money* (London: Macmillan, 1936).

the new lead society and contemporary modernity

increases in "service" and "white collar" occupations.[43] The second feature originated in Germany but has evolved farthest in the United States: the harnessing of scientific knowledge to industrial production. From the chemical and electrical industries it has spread to a wide range of others. Electronics, closely related to cybernetics and information processing, is perhaps the farthest-reaching development so far.

The American legal system has also favored economic growth. The Constitution prohibited tariffs and restrictions on the movement of people among the states at a time when Europe was much more fragmented by internal and interstate tariffs. The legal framework regulating property and contract was adopted from England but then was developed substantially farther, mostly through judicial decisions.[44] Later American lawyers pioneered in developing the private corporation, laying the legal groundwork for differentiation of ownership from managerial control.

An extensive system of occupational roles, based on employment rather than on proprietorship, was institutionalized in American society quite early and has spread with industrialization and urbanization. It involves differentiation between households and employing organizations, mainly business firms, though it also applies to employment in government and much of the private nonprofit sector. "Occupationalizing" of work in the early phases of modernization was generally restricted to employed "laborers" at the bottom of the occupational hierarchy. Later employment —and therefore the labor market—spread upward; it now includes, as executives (managerial or administrative) and professionals, most of the elements that were previously proprietary. This critical structural transformation is entirely overlooked in most comparisons of capitalism and socialism.[45]

In the fully modern phase, with the decline in the proportion of the labor force in agriculture, the primary contributions of adult males to larger functional interests of the society are, with few exceptions, made in occupational "jobs." Furthermore, the participation of women, particularly married women, in the labor force has also increased sharply.

Certain functions strongly resist "occupationalizing." They seem to reflect diffuse interests that would be threatened by the kind of specialization inherent in occupational roles. Their diffuseness may take in several systems. The family and household are central to both personality and organic concerns. Culture has been historically conspicuous in religious functions, but in the modern world it is also expressed by artists, who strongly resist "professionalizing." At the level of social system, aside

[43] Neil J. Smelser, *The Sociology of Economic Life* (Englewood Cliffs, N.J.: Prentice-Hall, 1964).
[44] Hurst, *Law and the Conditions of Freedom*.
[45] Talcott Parsons, *Structure and Process in Modern Societies*.

the new lead society and contemporary modernity

from the role of the politician, which we have already discussed, there are many both government and private "fiduciary" roles, like "trustees" of organizations that are not exclusively "profit making." For the individual citizen, however, fiduciary responsibility for the "public interest" becomes segmented; it involves his roles as voter and optional participant in communication processes and associations that further his views. Many categories of people are under strong pressure, psychological and otherwise, to become "engaged" to the point of giving their "causes" clear priority over their "jobs" or their families. These pressures are intensified in modern society by extensive and continuous change and attendant conflicts. Furthermore, the attainment of such limited goals as economic security and a fairly high standard of living opens vast possibilities for further improvements, to which strong emotions become attached. In social-psychological terms, our times are an age of unprecedented "relative deprivation."

A labor-union movement is prominent in every modern society. Structurally it is rooted in the "gap" between household and job that has been created by the spread of occupations. Its leaders have been not the most disadvantaged workers but those with higher levels of skills and social status, so that in some respects it is a successor to the craft guilds. Its primary strength, however, has been among manual workers and its primary orientation toward the protection and improvement of their economic interests and status. It has spread unevenly both among the most unskilled and among white-collar workers.

In the United States, especially since the New Deal, the union movement has acquired substantial strength in industry without providing a base for a political socialist movement as it has in most of Europe since the late nineteenth century. This anomaly reflects the extent to which American society was already "democratized," including opportunities for economic and social mobility.

There has been general and continuous upgrading within the occupational world. The proportion of the modern labor force that is composed of unskilled "laborers" has been shrinking. Historians of the industrial revolution long treated growth in physical volume of output, investment of money capital, and numbers employed in an industry as alternative general measures of productive growth, presuming that they varied in close proximity. But they have ceased to do so. Since the 1920s the total output of manufacturing industry in the United States has increased greatly, wheras the number employed in it has remained almost constant, and the proportion of the labor force employed in it has declined substantially.

This decline is primarily a result of "mechanization," now merging into "automation," and to improvements in organization, which have occasioned much "technological unemployment," as in the tragic example of the early nineteenth-century hand-loom weavers. There has been a progressive restriction of employment opportunities for those without fairly specific qualifications. This restriction has, however, produced not a permanently rising unemployment rate but a general rise in the competence of the labor force, resulting from educational upgrading. In the middle third of the present century the early phase of mass and assembly-line production placed a high premium on "semiskilled" labor, often to the detriment of older skilled craftsmen. Now more general levels of competence, which presume secondary-school education rather than particular skills, are increasingly required.

The development of occupational roles and the attendant emphasis upon performance have undermined the significance of ascriptive background conditions. Although "discrimination" by lineage membership, social class, ethnic origin, religion, race, and so on is tenacious, there seems to be steady and effective long-run pressure for evaluation—and thus admission to membership and achievement opportunities—on predominantly universalist grounds.[46]

Distribution of income among households is complex. The most important single factor is the labor market, which reflects differential demand for different services. Independent proprietorship has steadily declined, especially in agriculture. Wages and salaries, along with such forms of income as commissions, are broadly a function of competence and responsibility required in occupational roles, which are in turn increasingly influenced by education. Here it should be kept in mind that, because of increasing financial aid to higher education, the latter is no longer available mainly to children of the well-to-do.

Modification in the scale determined by demand for occupational services—some of the demand, as for academic professionals, is subsidized—occurs at both ends. In all modern societies massive "transfer payments" (as economists call them) subsidize the living standards of the lower-income groups through "relief," old-age security, unemployment benefits, health services, low-rent housing, and many other measures. A "floor"—below which it is felt no major category of people should fall—defines the minimum content of the "social" component of modern citizenship.[47] The pattern is uneven, as indicated by present concern over poverty in the United States. Nevertheless, the adoption of such a floor is characteristic of industrial societies in the twentieth century. Furthermore, transfer subsidies merge with measures to help otherwise handicapped individuals to "help themselves," most obviously through universal public education. Furthermore, largely under pressure from trade unions, increased wages

---

[46] Parsons, "A Revised Analytical Approach to the Theory of Social Stratification," and "Equality and Inequality in Modern Society . . . ," *Sociological Inquiry*, 40/2 (Spring 1970).

[47] Marshall, *op. cit.*

the new lead society and contemporary modernity

and growing "fringe benefits" have greatly improved the economic position of the so-called "working class."

The market is historically the locus classicus of competitive individualism, institutionalized in the full expectation that participation would lead to differential success. Most capitalist theory has thus focused only upon guaranteeing the fairness of competitive conditions, the pattern of equality of opportunity. There are many facets of the balance between equality and differential success as it has been continuously worked out since the eighteenth century. Not the least important phenomenon has been the increasing differentiation between the success status of the firm and the occupational status of the individual participating in the firm's productive activities.

Socialism, as we have remarked, has tended to set up a rigid alternative to the "free enterprise" market economy, advocating concentration of control of all major factors of production in central government. A principal demonstration that this alternative is not the only one lies in the establishment (just reviewed) in all "industrial" societies of some kind of "floor" of income and welfare open to all participants in the economy. We shall presently remark on some mechanisms that tend to counteract the more extreme tendencies to inequality in the other direction. We therefore suggest that here again there is a basic integrative "problem," of balancing the egalitarian component in modern values and those components of the "achievement complex" that engender differences of hierarchical status within the societal community. We shall comment briefly on the more general problem at the end of this chapter.

At the other end of the demand scale there is appreciable property income. To a very great extent, this income is dissociated from proprietorship. Rural landed proprietorship, the main politico-economic base of early modern aristocracies, has lost its importance. In the most recent phase the importance of business proprietorship has also declined, though much less drastically. The crucial form of property has come to be fluid, marketable monetary assets; corporate and government securities are the prototypes. In the United States property income is estimated at something over 20 percent of "personal" income, a proportion that seems not to have varied greatly for a generation or more.[48] Much of such property is in forms outside ordinary currently disposable income, for example, investments in private insurance. Another very important development is the extent to which property income goes to institutional rather than to individual holders such as to foundations, colleges and universities, hospitals, and other charitable organizations and endowment funds.

Although property income is heavily concentrated among the well-to-

[48] William Haber (ed.), *Labor in a Changing America* (New York: Basic Books, 1966).

do, there is wider participation in its nonproprietary forms than there was in the earlier phase of free-enterprise societies, extending especially to the upper middle class. The accumulation of wealth by the rich is substantially checked by progressive taxation of incomes and estates. In general, income distribution is much more nearly equal in the later phases of modern societies than it was in the earlier phases or is in most contemporary "underdeveloped" societies. What is true of income is probably even more true of opportunity, especially since the opening of higher education to increased proportions of each age group. Although the long-run stability of the current pattern is uncertain, the probable trend is toward greater equality still.

There is a curious counterpoint to these developments in criticism of the leading classes of modern society. On one hand, they are accused of having "gone soft"; on the other, they are accused of being too absorbed in the "narrow" interests of their work. Although all such accusations invite suspicion, the latter seems realistic. Occupationalizing and professionalizing management have entailed immense upgrading of educational standards, expectations, and average attainment, requiring high motivation to achieve among participants. The widespread motivational commitment necessary was probably not present during earlier phases of our social development. Despite certain reductions in the hours of formal work and perhaps a slackening of effort in some types of work, commitment to occupational performance remains high. Very likely it has been increasing, particularly at the highest occupational levels. The upper occupational groups in modern society, far from constituting a "leisure class" are generally among the most intensely "working" groups in human history. Paradoxically, the allegedly "exploited" working class has moved far closer to becoming the leisure class of modern society. The hard work of the upper groups does not consist mainly of muscular exertion or adherence to stringent supervisory discipline; rather it involves solving difficult, often baffling, problems and taking responsibility for solutions.

There has been a general raising of standards of nutrition, clothing, housing, and other components of the standard of living. Only in the lowest brackets of the modern poor is there such *drastic* deprivation—to the point of near starvation, considerably lower life expectancy, ragged clothing, and the like—as characterizes much of the "underdeveloped" world today. This problem clearly is not the same as that of the incidence of such "social pathologies" as drug addiction.

There has also been a general upgrading in expressive standards, as demonstrated by rising consumption of "cultural goods" and by related levels of aesthetic taste in household furnishings, food, and the like (including participation in public recreation). Even though previously disadvantaged or isolated groups have often fostered aesthetic monstrosities that older and later upper groups have not been slow to ridicule, it seems that

112

the new lead society and contemporary modernity

"sophisticated" tastes are probably shared by a substantially larger proportion of the population in modern societies than ever before. This development is difficult to evaluate, however. On one hand, increased consumption is apt to be disapproved by "puritans," who regard it as evidence that the current generation is "going soft." On the other, *Gemeinschaft* romanticists allege that the taste of simple people has everywhere been corrupted by modernization.

Another prominent theme in the discussion of standards of living in "affluent" societies is competition for status through "conspicuous consumption," extending from the ostentatious entertainment and palaces of the old aristocracies to the rather modest contemporary "keeping up with the Joneses." Some such competitiveness is probably unavoidable when standards of universalism and achievement are institutionalized. Yet it seems that the decline of the aristocracy has reduced the importance of invidious consumption differences. For example, the White House, though hardly a log cabin, is far from being another Palace of Versailles. The Gilded Age mansions of New York's Fifth Avenue and Newport are either disappearing or being turned over to "public" use; similar trends are apparent in Europe. Probably in most modern countries "bourgeois" ostentation is now considerably less extreme than it was in the eighteenth or the nineteenth centuries, though there is much broader enjoyment of some kinds of "luxuries." As "conspicuous consumption" is not new and has almost certainly declined at the extremes, it is difficult to see in modern luxury consumption a primary symptom of the decadence of modern society.[49]

An associated development is the "capitalization" of "consumers' durable" goods, including the dwelling and such equipment as central heating, "appliances," and furniture. Privacy is also important in the modern standard of living—a "room of one's own" for the married couple and for all but quite young children is now taken for granted.

These developments are partly a consequence, partly a determinant, of an important change in class structure, the reduction in the "servant class." Early in the present century the typical "middle class" home had one domestic servant "living in," where as to be "upper middle class" required a considerable staff. Today only the very rich have a staff of servants, a large proportion by virtue of some institutional position. The upper middle-class household generally operates with a "cleaning woman" one or two days a week and baby-sitters.

There are two other reasons for this development. First, modern industry has become increasingly capital-intensive, making labor the scarcest factor and thus increasingly expensive—the reciprocal of the general rise

---

[49] Perry Miller shows that Americans had much the same concern with decadent affluence in the seventeenth and eighteenth centuries as they have now. See *Nature's Nation* (Cambridge, Mass.: Harvard University Press, 1967).

in the standard of living. Second, increasing egalitarianism has stigmatized the status of servant,[50] making employment in factories or stores increasingly preferable to domestic service.

These developments have not been without cost to the middle-class married woman. Deprived of household help and subject to increasing demands in the emotional management of family relations, in the broader range of citizenship, and increasingly in occupations as well, she relies upon an array of modern household appliances that is not sheer extravagance.

Conclusion

The United States' new type of societal community, more than any other single factor, justifies our assigning it the lead in the latest phase of modernization. We have suggested that it synthesizes to a high degree the equality of opportunity stressed in socialism. It presupposes a market system, a strong legal order relatively independent of government, and a "nation-state" emancipated from specific religious and ethnic control. The educational revolution has been considered as a crucial innovation, especially with regard to the emphasis on the associational pattern, as well as on openness of opportunity. Above all, American society has gone farther than any comparable large-scale society in its dissociation from the older ascriptive inequalities and the institutionalization of a basically egalitarian pattern.

Contrary to the opinion among many intellectuals, American society —and most modern societies without dictatorial regimes—has institutionalized a far broader range of freedoms than had any previous society. This range is perhaps not greater than that sometimes enjoyed by such small privileged groups as eighteenth-century European aristocracy, but it is certainly broader than ever before for large masses of people.

There are many complexities attached to such freedoms. Perhaps they can be said to begin with freedom from some of the exigencies of physical life: ill health, short life, geographical circumscription, and the like. They certainly include reduced exposure to violence for most of the population most of the time. Higher incomes and extensive markets enhance freedom of choice in consumption. Then there is an immense range of free access to various services like education, public accommodations, and the like. There is widespread freedom of marital choice, of occupation, of religious adherence, of political allegiance, of thought, of speech and expression.

---

[50] Vilhelm Aubert, "The Housemaid: an Occupational Role in Crisis," in S. M. Lipset and N. J. Smelser (eds.), *Sociology: The Progress of a Decade* (Englewood Cliffs, N.J.: Prentice-Hall, 1961).

the new lead society and contemporary modernity

From a broad comparative and evolutionary perspective, the more "privileged" societies of the later twentieth century have to an impressive degree, which would have been impossible to predict a century ago, successfully institutionalized the more "liberal" and "progressive" values of that time.

There are of course important flaws. One surely is war and the danger of war. As we are dealing here with the nature of the societal community, however, we shall postpone discussion of intersocietal relations to the concluding chapter of this book.

We have already suggested that the primary deficiencies of the new societal community type do not lie in the older grievances against the tyranny of authoritarian regimes, especially of the monarchical variety, or the entrenched privileges of aristocracies. Nor do they apparently lie in class antagonism and exploitation in the strict Marxian sense. The problems of inequality and social justice remain salient, but framing these problems in simple terms of bourgeoisie versus proletariat is, for reasons that have been reviewed in this chapter, no longer relevant.

There is one clear context, however, in which the equality-justice problem is central in the United States: the existence of substantial poverty in combination with the large Negro minority that has suffered a long history of discrimination originating in slavery. It is important to be clear that the two aspects of the problem do not coincide completely. By most criteria the substantial majority of the American poor is white, and there is a substantial nonwhite population that is not poor. There is, however, an especially striking coincidence of the two among "ghetto" blacks in the central cities.

The older view of these problems stresses "absolute" deprivation, malnutrition, disease, and the like. The conviction that *relative* deprivation is more important, that what "hurts" most is the sense of *exclusion* from full participation in the societal community has, however, been growing among social scientists.[51] In our general paradigm of social change we have stressed the connection between inclusion and adaptive upgrading—through rising income—but they are not identical. The connection does, however, help to explain why, considering the very great recent reduction of legal and political discrimination, tensions over the race problem have intensified rather than subsiding. That mitigation of feelings of relative deprivation through inclusion is in a sense "symbolic" does not make it one bit the less urgent and important.

In a second context, the problem of equality and social justice is more difficult to assess. As just noted, the older grievances of tyranny entrenched

---

[51] See Lee Rainwater and William Yancey, *The Moynihan Report and the Politics of Controversy* (Cambridge, Mass.: M.I.T. Press, 1967); and Talcott Parsons and Kenneth Clark (eds.), *The Negro American* (Boston: Houghton-Mifflin, 1966).

the new lead society and contemporary modernity

privilege, and class in the Marxian sense are less central than they once were. But there still remains a pervasive sense that specially advantaged groups use their positions illegitimately to promote their own interests at the expense of the common interest. In an earlier generation these grievances were most likely to be defined in economic terms, as in Franklin D. Roosevelt's reference to "malefactors of great wealth." Significantly, the tendency now is to invoke the symbol of "power"—in C. W. Mills' phrase, a "power élite" is now held responsible for most of our social ills. Members of the power élite are less likely to be defined as office holders than as sinister wire pullers behind the scenes. Ideological complexes with paranoid themes are very old indeed, but the question of what lies behind this particular one nevertheless arises.

Indignation over the economic privileges of the rich does not seem to be a major source of the general moral malaise in modern society; indeed, it seems less so that it was at the turn of the century. There is a virtually unanimous consensus that those elements below the "poverty line" should be brought above it. Beyond that consensus the problem of economic inequality becomes very complicated. It seems that the long-range trend has been one of reduction in "conspicuous consumption" among the highest groups. Though not much has happened for a generation, it is likely that the future trend will be toward greater equalization.

In terms of power and authority, society has on balance become more decentralized and associational, rather than more concentrated. This trend again suggests an explanation in terms of relative rather than absolute deprivation. "Bureaucracy," has become a particularly prominent negative symbol, implying as it does stringent centralized control through rigid rules and authority. We have argued that the main trend is actually not toward increased bureaucracy, even if bureaucracy itself were not in process of transformation, but rather toward associationism. But many sensitive groups clearly *feel* that bureaucracy has been increasing. This sense is also related to recent waves of accusation against the "military-industrial complex" in the United States, which in turn is associated with a pervasive sense of limitation on freedom; in the most extreme circles the gains in freedoms that we have summarized are virtually denied.

There are in the expression of this sense of deprivation two especially prominent positive symbols. One is "community," which is widely alleged to have grossly deteriorated in the course of modern developments.[52] It is pointed out that the residential community has been "privatized" and that many relationships have been shifted to the context of large formal organizations. We should note again, however, that bureaucratization in its

[52] One form is the nostalgia for *Gemeinschaft*, which has been a prominent feature of the "sociological tradition," especially as portrayed by Robert Nisbet, *The Sociological Tradition* (New York: Basic Books, 1967).

116

the new lead society and contemporary modernity

most pejorative sense is not threatening to sweep all before it. Furthermore, the whole system of mass communications is a functional equivalent of some features of *Gemeinschaft* society and one that enables an individual selectively to participate according to his own standards and desires.[53] The second positive symbol is "participation," especially in the formula of "participatory democracy." Demands for it are often stated as if "power," in a specific technical sense, were the main desideratum, but the very diffuseness of these demands casts doubt on this conclusion. We suggest that the demands are mainly another manifestation of the desire for inclusion, for full "acceptance" as members of solidary groups. Similar considerations seem applicable to the abhorrence and fear of *illegitimate* power. Just what form desirable participation can take compatible with the exigencies of effective organization is a matter of great complexity, but this focus of tension seems clear.

Perhaps some confirmation of this interpretation can be derived from the prominence throughout modern societies in recent years of extreme student unrest associated, as we have suggested, with the development of mass higher education. This phenomenon is too complex to be analyzed here, but it is suggestive that the themes stressed by student radicals have more general resonance in society at large. Both negatively and positively power is a potent symbol; the "wrong" kind of power allegedly explains most of what is "wrong" in society, and "student power" is prominent among the remedies advocated. Bureaucracy and related themes are associated with the "wrong"kind of power. On the positive side a new concept of "community," with respect to which participation is strongly stressed, is endowed with almost magical virtues.[54]

We have in this book stressed the importance in modern society of three "revolutions." Each has been a center of tension and conflict, producing radical groups that have opposed both certain features of the social structure that is in flux and the revolutionary changes. The French Revolution, the most prominent single phase of the early democratic revolution, thus spawned the Jacobins, the "absolutists" of Rousseauean democracy. The industrial revolution, somewhat later, generated conflicts about which we have had a good deal to say; the socialists, especially the communist wing, were the radicals of this phase. It may not be too far-fetched to suggest that the student radicals of the New Left have begun to play an ana-

---

[53] Surely the main orientation of sociology is not toward restoring the societies that preceded the industrial and democratic revolutions, or even the educational revolution. Rather it has been toward a search for those components of social systems that have accounted for some of the positive features of earlier societies, with a view toward understanding how they can be reshaped to meet the functional exigencies of emerging modern societies. See Edward A. Shils, "Mass Society and Its Culture," *Daedalus* (Spring 1960); and Winston White, *Beyond Conformity* (New York: Free Press, 1961).

[54] For a discussion on this point, see Parsons and Platt, *op. cit.*, p. 26.

logous role in the educational revolution—though how many phases are still to come we do not know.

At this point we face what seems to be a paradox. Of all people, revolutionaries most resent hearing that they share any values with those whose "immoral" systems they seek to overthrow. As we have used the concept of values in analysis, however, it is legitimate to raise the question whether or not the basic value *patterns* of modern society, and especially of the United States, are being fundamentally challenged. Are the institutional achievements associated with "liberal progressive" values of the nineteenth century no longer relevant? Have they been repudiated by the new generation?

The answer clearly is no. These values tend to be taken for granted, not repudiated.[55] On one hand, modern society is indicted for not living up to its professed values, as demonstrated by the existence of poverty and racial discrimination and the persistence of war and imperialism. On the other, there is a vague insistence that society should not be content with these value implementations but should introduce altogether new ones.

Egalitarian themes are very prominent in definitions of what the next phases should be, and the two symbols of community and participation at least point in certain directions, however unclear their implications may be in detail. The modern system, particularly in the United States, seems to have just completed one phase of institutional consolidation, but it is also undergoing the ferment that accompanies the emergence of new phases, the shape of which cannot yet be clearly discerned.

One thing that does seem clear is the strategic significance of the societal community in such situations. As has been suggested, the emergence of the most important features of this community is quite recent. Furthermore, there is every reason to believe both that the United States has led the change and that the main features will spread through all modern societies. A somewhat fuller description of these features is therefore in order.

The principle of equality has broken through to a new level of pervasiveness and generality. A societal community as *basically* composed of

[55] One conspicuous objection to this statement is obvious: The more extreme student radicals resort to the revolutionary tactic of "confrontation," including the use of violence and all manner of devices to deny what liberals consider a fair hearing for those whose positions they oppose; deliberate disruption of academic discussions is a case in point. This behavior is a repudiation in practice of what we may call the "procedural" values of "liberal" society; it is often defended most vociferously as necessary because of the repressive character of the "Establishment." At the same time it should be noted that people who engage in such tactics repeatedly invoke *their* "rights" in a way that clearly precludes their having repudiated these liberal values. Furthermore, it is conspicuous that this trait is common to *all* extreme radicals and not only to current ones. The Terror under the Jacobins was hardly "democratic," yet it was perpetrated in the name of democracy. Communist tactics in our own time have been similar. This conflict between supposed ultimate values like equality and freedom and the tactics of radicalism is built into extreme radical movements.

118

the new lead society and contemporary modernity

equals seems to be the "end of the line" in the long process of undermining the legitimacy of such older, more particularistic ascriptive bases of membership as religion (in pluralistic society), ethnic affiliation, region or locality, and hereditary position in social stratification (notably in the aristocracy but also more recent versions of class status). This basic theme of equality has long antecedents but was first crystallized in conceptions of "natural rights" under the Enlightenment and found particularly important expression in the Bill of Rights of the American Constitution. The Bill of Rights has proved to be a kind of time bomb, as some of its consequences have emerged only long after its official adoption, most dramatically through Supreme Court action but also more generally. The current prominence of poverty and race problems in the United States is largely owing to the deep moral repugnance that the conception of an inherently "lower" class, to say nothing of an inferior race, arouses in modern societies, despite vociferous objections to modern egalitarianism among certain groups.

Some widespread current radical ideologies seem to demand that genuine equality requires total abolition of all hierarchical status distinctions. This version of "community" has been a persistently recurring ideal for many centuries. Such close approximations to realistic institutionalization as have occurred, however, have always been on a small scale and for the most part of rather short duration. It seems that too intensive a drive in this direction would be seriously disruptive of such larger-scale institutions of modern societies as law, markets, effective government, and competent creation and use of advanced knowledge. It would likely shatter society into an indefinite number of truly "primitive" small communities.

The main direction of modern societal development is toward an essentially new pattern of stratification. The primary historical bases of legitimate inequality have, as we have stressed, been ascriptive. The value base of the new egalitarianism, however, requires a different basis of legitimation. In general terms this basis must be *functional* in the society conceived as a system. Differential outcomes of the competitive educational process must thus be legitimated in terms of societal interest in the contributions of especially competent people; special competence is at least a function of both high native ability and "good training." There is also a societal interest in high economic productivity with no presumption that every individual or collective unit that participates will be equally productive, special rewards for the economically more productive units thus become necessary. Similarly, effective organization is a functional necessity of large and complex collectivities, and one of the prime factors in such effectiveness is the institutionalization of authority and power, which has an inherently differential aspect, the relative "concentration" of power. There are two main modes of reconciliation between the value im-

the new lead society and contemporary modernity

peratives of basic equality and of functional needs for competence, productivity, and collective effectiveness—all of which, of course, intersect in concrete areas of the social structure. The first mode is the institutionalization of *accountability*, the most familiar example of which is the accountability of elected officials to their constituencies. Economic markets perform certain analogous functions, though imperfectly, as do mechanisms for certifying competence in the academic world, the professions, and certain other "fiduciary" bodies.

The second mode is focused in the institutionalization of equality of opportunity, so that no citizen shall, for familiar ascriptive reasons (race, social class, religion, ethnic affiliation, and the like), be barred from equal access to opportunities for performance, as in employment, or to opportunities for making effective performance possible, like health and education. This ideal is, of course, very far from full realization, but the view, so prevalent today, that equality of opportunity is sheer "mockery" demonstrates that it is in fact being taken far more seriously than ever before. In earlier times the "lower classes," or individuals disadvantaged on other ascriptive bases, simply took for granted that opportunities open to "their betters" were "not for them," and they did not protest. The volume of protest is thus not a simple function of the magnitude of the "evil."

It is clear that balancing value-commitments to equality on one hand and inequalities implied in functional effectiveness on the other present complex integration problems to modern societies, especially as so many of the historic bases of hierarchical legitimation are no longer available. This difficulty is further compounded by the appearance of the problem not in one overarching sphere but in many very different spheres. There are many bases for functional inequality; the classification "competence–economic efficiency–collective effectiveness" constitutes only a most elementary framework. There must be integration not only between claims to special prerogatives and the principles of equality but also among different kinds of claims to special prerogatives in a highly pluralistic social system.

This integration is the focus of emerging institutions of stratification. In our opinion, none of the inherited formulas purporting to describe modern stratification is satisfactory. The basis is surely not, except in very special, limited, and ever fewer instances, in ethnic membership. It is neither aristocracy in the older sense nor class in the Marxian sense. It is, however, still incompletely developed and essentially new.

The integration of such a societal community must depend upon special mechanisms. They center around the attachment of highly generalized prestige not only to specific groups but also to the statuses that they occupy, including office in the sense of the bearers of authority in collectivities. It is essential that the prestige of such groups and statuses be

the new lead society and contemporary modernity

rooted in varying combinations of factors rather than in any one, like wealth, political power, or even "moral" authority. We define prestige as the "communication node" through which various factors essential to the integration of the societal community can be evaluated, balanced, and integrated in an output that we may call *influence*. The exercise of influence by one unit or set of units can then help to bring other units into some kind of consensus by justifying allocations of rights and obligations, expected performances, and rewards in terms of their contributions to a common interest. At our present level of reference, the common interest could be that of the society conceived of as a community.

The concentration on the societal community that has characterized this book as a whole and the present chapter in particular should be balanced by recognition that values always potentially, and usually actually, transcend *any* such particular community. That is one reason why this book has been concerned with the system of modern societies, rather with any one such society. The forces and processes that have transformed the societal community of the United States and promise to continue to transform it are not peculiar to this one society but permeate the whole modern—and "modernizing"—system. Only on such bases is it understandable that European societies with no racial problems of their own can feel justified in taunting Americans about their callousness in the treatment of blacks or small independent countries in raising outcries of "imperialism." From this point of view, the *intersocietal* institutionalization of a new value system, including its relevance to stratification, becomes crucial.

The salient foci of tension and conflict, and thus of creative innovation, in the current situation do not seem to be mainly economic in the sense of the nineteenth-century controversy over capitalism and socialism, nor do they seem political in the sense of the problem of the "justice" of the distribution of power, though both these conflicts are present. A cultural focus, especially in the wake of the educational revolution, is nearer the mark. The strong indications are, however, that the storm center is the societal community. On one hand, there is the relative obsolesence of many older values like hereditary privilege, ethnicity and class. On the other, there are unsolved problems of integrating the normative structure of community, which seems fairly complete in outline, with the motivational basis of solidarity, which remains much more problematic. The new societal community, conceived as an integrative institution, must operate at a level different from those familiar in our intellectual traditions; it must go beyond command of political power and wealth and of the factors that generate them to value commitments and mechanisms of influence.

new counterpoints

seven

To many readers, the attention to American society in the preceding chapter may seem parochial. But it seemed that the emerging pattern could be best delineated through discussion of one example at some length rather than of several much more briefly. The United States was selected out of conviction that it has become—for how long remains to be seen—the leader of the modern system, *not* in the usual political sense but through structural innovations central to the main course of modern societal development. This choice was based upon the evolutionary scheme that we have been following in this book as a whole. We have stressed the broad trend of development in a more "individualistic," decentralized, and associational direction, beginning as far back as feudalism, as discussed by Bloch. If our judgment was sound in Chapter 4 in selecting the "northwest corner" of Europe as the "leading" sector for the seventeenth-century crystallization, parallel considerations suggest a similar role for the United States in the most recent phase; comparable patterns are also clear in such related societies as those of Canada and Australia.[1] This perspective develops from the picture of American society

[1] See S. M. Lipset, *The First New Nation* (New York: Basic Books, 1963).

122

presented by Tocqueville in the 1830s, when its potential was just becoming apparent to the discerning observer. This trend appears to offer a more reliable clue than do more recent pictures of American society as characterized above all by bureaucratization and concentration of power.

Let us now outline the modern system generally. We argue that, as in the early modern phase, the "lead" elements emphasize goal attainment *for the system* but adaptation and integration *within* the system. These twin emphases characterized England and Holland in the seventeenth century and the United States in the twentieth. They reflect the general development of the modern system in the direction of adaptation and associational emphases. The other primary innovative function *for the system* is adaptive. The units that have emphasized the adaptive function of the system—Prussia in the early phase and now the Soviet Union—have emphasized societal goal attainment of the particular society.

This apparent paradox is perhaps best resolved by reference to concrete examples. We imputed to Prussia the extension and consolidation of predominantly Western patterns on the system's northeastern frontier and the establishment of a structural basis for unification of Germany. These processes engendered very severe conflicts when Germany was integrated into the more associational and democratic structure of Western Europe, but a reorganized Germany then led the economic modernization of the Continent.

Like Prussia, the Soviet Union has "extended" the European system eastward. From the late eighteenth century on Russia moved increasingly into the European system, particularly in the wars against the French Revolution and Napoleon and in stabilizing the subsequent "conservative" settlement. During the nineteenth century it extended European society to the Pacific Ocean through colonization of Siberia.

There is one major implication of attributing the primary sources of innovation in the more recent phases of the modern system to the goal-attainment and adaptive subsystems. This is the presumption, which has not been fully worked out and justified in this brief book, that there has been since the Renaissance and the Reformation a broad general stability in the main *patterns* of value orientation that have become institutionalized.[2] There have, of course, been innumerable conflicts over values, but by and large these conflicts have occurred at levels of specification below that of the most general. It is also very important that each of the main steps in differentiation and the other processes of change that have been traced has stimulated and partly been shaped by changes in the level of generality of the value pattern. A conspicuous example is the change

[2] See Talcott Parsons, "Christianity," in *International Encyclopedia of the Social Sciences* (New York: Macmillan, 1968).

that permitted religious freedom in place of the older Christian tradition of established churches and enforced religious uniformity.

Both the United States and the Soviet Union have had ideologies varying from older Western European patterns; some, especially the Soviet, are still partially repudiated by Western European societies. But the value content of these ideologies should, in our opinion, be regarded as primarily "specifications" of the more general Western value pattern of instrumental activism, rather than as departures from it. In general, the same can be said of the ideologies of "social criticism" and revolt that are widely current in our time.

The Soviet Union

As the Russian Revolution took shape after the chaos created by collapse of the war effort, civil war, and international intervention, firm political control went to the "dictatorship of the proletariat," the special communist variant of socialism. The party and the government became agencies of modernization as much as of revolutionary conquest.

Although industrialization had begun in Russia before the Revolution of 1917—some authorities argue that the Revolution actually slowed its pace[3]—massive efforts at development were first launched by the Soviet regime. Of the two revolutions of the early modernizing period, the Soviet Union's more striking success has been in industrialization; in a short time it has attained the second position in the world.

The Soviet regime has also, however, introduced many features of the democratic revolution, despite its primarily dictatorial character. Many ascriptive components of the older society have been eliminated: The monarchy was immediately abolished; the aristocracy, which had been more tightly linked to the throne even than in France, was wiped out as a status group; for a considerable time the children of bourgeois and aristocrats were so systematically discriminated against that there is now a predominantly new "upper class."[4]

The identification of the Russian Church with the czarist regime was closer than any church-state relationship in Western Europe. The communist movement followed the French Revolution in its radical anticlericalism and carried it farther than had any noncommunist nation. The older position of the Church has been destroyed, and organized

---

[3] See Alexander Gerschenkron, "Problems and Patterns of Russian Economic Development," in C. E. Black (ed.), *The Transformation of Russian Society* (Cambridge, Mass: Harvard University Press, 1960).

[4] Merle Fainsod, *How Russia Is Ruled* (rev. ed., Cambridge, Mass.: Harvard University Press, 1963).

124

religion enjoys very limited toleration. Marxism-Leninism has attained semi-religious status, however, which obstructs religious pluralism.

Industrialization has vastly reduced traditional localism and particularism. Urbanization, education, geographical mobility, and status mobility have all increased greatly, even though freedom of movement and employment are relatively restricted.[5]

These processes indicate a shift toward citizenship within the societal community. At certain levels, the Soviet system stresses universalistic standards and strives to qualify all its citizenry for full inclusion, through both general education and indoctrination in established beliefs. Yet even more than the French Revolution, Soviet policy confronts a dilemma between tight control by party and government and maximization of freedom, the expressed ideal of the "withering away of the state." One focus of the problem is on institutions intermediate between the central authority and the masses of the people.

Many institutions that were formerly opposed, though in varying degrees, by the Communist Party have regained fairly open acceptability. One is inequality of occupational income, reflecting, as in other societies, competence and responsibility. Another is the family. After a period when divorce was available upon request, it became more difficult to secure than in most capitalist societies.[6] Related to both is permission for individuals and families to hold some private financial resources in the form of savings accounts and the like.[7] Similarly, adjudication independent of administrative authority, though restricted, has become significant.[8] Although such institutions are now accepted, there is still much uneasiness about their scope and autonomy, as, for example, in parents' control over their children.

The government's administration of the economy has been a central issue. In the Stalinist phase of five-year plans, military insecurity, and war, concentration of authority was extreme. It was the era of political totalitarianism and the "command economy."[9] Economic development was extraordinary up to a point, but, as the Great Purge of the late 1930s demonstrated, it was accompanied by severe political strains, of which the "de-Stalinization" crisis of the middle 1950s was an aftermath.

The command economy suppressed or severely limited many of the

---

[5] Alex Inkeles and Raymond A. Bauer, The Soviet Citizen (Cambridge, Mass.: Harvard University Press, 1959).

[6] See Kent Geiger, The Family in Soviet Russia (Cambridge, Mass.: Harvard University Press, 1969).

[7] See Inkeles and Bauer, op. cit.

[8] See Harold J. Berman, Justice in the U.S.S.R. (rev. ed.; Cambridge, Mass.: Harvard University Press, 1963).

[9] See Gregory Grossman, "The Structure and Organization of the Soviet Economy," Slavic Review, 21 (June 1962), 203–22.

principal mechanisms of other industrial economies, most obviously money and markets.[10] A system of hierarchial decisions was substituted for the market. Plant managers implemented the instructions of the central planning authority, using the materials and manpower allocated to them from other centrally controlled units.[11] Many difficulties resulted from such radical centralization, and the Soviets are still attempting to reduce it without compromising socialist principles. The allocation of manpower is particularly sensitive because a policy of assignment so radically restricts individual freedom. Soviet practice is now far from a quasi-military ordering of people to particular jobs. But the same basic problem appears in consumption. Although Soviet planners often deride capitalist "consumer sovereignty," they have had increasingly to tailor production plans to what consumers find at least acceptable, especially since recent increases in consumer income [12] have initiated what Rostow calls the phase of "mass consumption." [13]

Probably the most serious problem remains the demarcation between the rights of government and citizen. From the Western point of view, the totalitarian phase, symbolized by terror and the secret police, denied the "rights of the citizen" enforceable *against* government.[14] Since Stalin's death its rigor has been greatly relaxed, though how firmly rooted civil rights are remains uncertain. Ideologically individual freedoms are supposed to become nearly absolute with the advent of communism, but practically it is not clear how they are to do so.

Whereas the Soviet Union has institutionalized the franchise, it essentially applies only to "yes-no" choices, permitting no organized opposition to the incumbent leadership. Although it fails to present the average citizen with genuine choice about the general direction of governmental policy, it nevertheless does differ from the older European "legitimacy" that treated individuals as the subjects of their monarchs.[15]

From these beginnings political citizenship more like the general Western pattern may develop. A Stalinist type of dictatorship is apparently no longer possible. At least the leadership probably now requires endorsement by the Central Committee of the Communist Party, which can no

[10] See Gregory Grossman, *Economic Systems* (Englewood Cliffs, N.J.: Prentice-Hall, 1967).
[11] Joseph S. Berliner, *Factory and Manager in the U.S.S.R.* (Cambridge, Mass.: Harvard University Press, 1957).
[12] Marshall I. Goldman, *The Soviet Economy* (Englewood Cliffs, N.J.: Prentice-Hall, 1968).
[13] Walt W. Rostow, *The Stages of Economic Growth* (Cambridge, Mass.: Harvard University Press, 1960).
[14] Barrington Moore, Jr., *Terror and Progress: U.S.S.R.* (Cambridge, Mass.: Harvard University Press, 1954).
[15] See Alex Inkeles, *Public Opinion in Soviet Russia* (Cambridge, Mass.: Harvard University Press, 1950).

new counterpoints

longer be ignored or manipulated as it was by Stalin. This system may evolve toward an approximate equivalent of the British parliamentary system of the eighteenth century.

The social component of Soviet citizenship has become highly developed. Although it is embedded in far more hierarchial, bureaucratic, and authoritarian structures than exist in the main Western societies, it shows how far the Soviet Union has evolved from seventeenth-century absolutism.[16]

There are instabilities inherent in the dictatorship of the Communist Party. The party, and therefore its leadership, is *self*-appointed. The nearest parallel seems to be the "saints" of Calvinist polities, including early New England. In each instance the legitimating cultural tradition has given no universal criterion defining *who* is qualified for the élite. The Soviet system does not recognize legitimation by birth, the classic stabilizer of aristocratic systems. To the degree that the party succeeds in "educating" the population as good socialists, there should emerge strong democratizing pressures parallel to those that developed in Western polities and in Protestantism for eliminating the special status of an elect.

We suggest, then, that the processes of the democratic revolution have not yet reached an equilibrium in the Soviet Union and that further developments *may* well run broadly in the direction of Western types of democratic government, with responsibility to an electorate rather than to a self-appointed party.

Although formal education at all levels had been available to a relatively small minority before the Revolution, one of the first great Soviet efforts was to advance mass education. The result has been that the Soviet people are now among the most widely educated in the modern world. They have also extended the levels of education upward faster than has almost any society except the United States and Canada. Physical science and technology have been emphasized, largely because of the drive toward rapid industrialization and military considerations, as well as the relative safety of these fields in ideological terms. Ideological indoctrination has been very prominent in higher education and has shaped the humanities and social sciences to a considerable extent. Prominent in current disaffection with the regime are literary intellectuals and artists, who suffer from seriously repressive measures.

Soviet research is concentrated in academies of sciences separate from the universities. A related organizational feature is control of training in the professions by the respective ministries rather than by universities: For example, medical schools are under the Ministry of Health, rather than the Ministry of Education. It seems probable that the major reasons

[16] Inkeles and Bauer, *op. cit.*

for this organizational pattern are political. The academy system insulates research from the more "public" sectors of the society, giving research personnel greater freedom than they could have if the broader social repercussions of their work were to be more directly controlled.

The establishment of new communist regimes in Eastern Europe after World War II and then in China ended "socialism in one country." The European socialist societies have not constituted an "iron curtain" but a permeable boundary vis-à-vis Western noncommunist influences. This boundary, along with such channels as broadcasting, publications, and visits in both directions, has affected the Soviet system in important ways.

Before World War II the boundary countries were generally more "European" than was Russia. Not surprisingly, they have shown stronger liberalizing trends, in the Western sense, though sporadically and unevenly. Whereas the Soviets have occasionally taken strong measures to repress movements toward autonomy in Eastern Europe—as in Hungary in 1956 Czechoslovakia in 1968,—the long-run impact on the Soviet system itself will probably, though by no means certainly, favor liberalization. In some ways, the cost to the Soviet Union of maintaining its "empire" parallels the cost to many capitalist powers of coping with independence movements in their former colonies.

Communist China has raised the first serious challenge to Soviet leadership of "world" communism, engendering severe tensions that few would have anticipated several years ago. This challenge may push the Soviet Union toward certain accommodations with the West, though it is counterbalanced by commitments to maintaining unity within the communist movement.

In the first post-Stalin phase of Soviet communism, Khrushchev introduced the formula of peaceful coexistence, a striking parallel to *cuius regio, eius religio*, the formula that ended the wars of religion. It also represented negative toleration: The foreign ideological adversary was no longer to be fought with force, but no concessions on the legitimacy of its ideological position were to be allowed. Perhaps, despite American involvement in Vietnam, the "hot" phase of the cold war is coming to an end. If the parallel with the earlier religious situation is valid, however, "peaceful coexistence" is not a stable stopping place. The development will probably continue through many vicissitudes toward an ideologically more "ecumenical" situation.

The "New Europe" [17]

There have been turbulent developments at the European core of the modern system: two world wars, the first spawning

[17] For a general discussion, see Stephen R. Graubard (ed.), *A New Europe?* (Boston: Houghton Mifflin, 1964).

new counterpoints

the Russian Revolution and the Fascist movements, the second sealing the doom of the "imperial" status of the European powers and shifting leadership to the United States and the Soviet Union.

Perhaps the most suitable single formulation of Europe's main line of development is "Americanization," a term frequently used pejoratively by European intellectuals. We hope to set aside here not only this evaluation but also the question of how much the changes result from American "influence" and how much from indigenous developments, though surely the latter are of substantial importance. In certain respects, the ideological reaction to "Americanization" is analogous to the Counter-Reformation or the conservative alliance against the effects of the French Revolution. The Reformation, the democratic revolution, and we think, "Americanization" have all been processes of irreversible change in Western society as a whole.

The Continental center of gravity moved to France and the new Germany after 1870. Despite acute conflicts between them, together they still constitute the main pattern-maintenance base of the emerging "New Europe," and of the modern system as a whole, although this base has since World War II extended to include northern Italy. The new north-central base was of mixed religious composition. Despite severe conflicts like the *Kulturkampf* in Germany and that between clericals and anti-clericals in France, this composition has favored religious pluralism, as has the weakening of the papacy by the largely secular state in Italy.

France, the original focus of the democratic revolution, lagged behind in the industrial revolution; a high proportion of its labor force remained in agriculture and small proprietary enterprise. Aristocracy, regionalism; the statuses of upper bourgeois, worker, and peasant, and other ascriptive components remained prominent. The nonascriptive integration of the societal community, which developed farthest in the United States, did not progress nearly so far in France.[18] The system of higher education and higher secondary education (the *lycées*) was until recently geared to the humanistic education of a very small élite, drawn mainly from the upper bourgeoisie.

Gaullism has perhaps served as a mild functional equivalent of the Nazi movement. It has emphasized nationalism, partly in compensation for the humiliation of 1940 and the loss of the French colonial empire, and has been economically conservative, especially in its concern with the international monetary position of France. But the processes of economic stabilization and revival after a generation and more of inflation have brought new inequalities. Above all, the working classes have not shared equally in the growing national income.

Compared to France, Germany industrialized rapidly before World

[18] See Stanley Hoffman et al., *In Search of France* (Cambridge, Mass.: Harvard University Press, 1963).

129

War I. This rapidity, however, put immense strains on its poorly integrated societal community, which was split religiously, regionally, and in other ways.[19] Although Germany pioneered in social security and was the seat of active trade-union and socialist movements, its democratic revolution was delayed and its opportunities for higher education restricted. The system of social stratification preserved many of the old elements of ascriptive inequality and diversity. These factors, combined with the defeat of World War I, sudden but unstable political democratization, and the rise of Soviet communism, provided the background for the Nazi eruption.

The internal structure of the German societal community, rather than the competition among great powers, was the most important focus of the strains behind Nazism, as evinced by the adoption of the Jew as the main negative symbol, the drive to incorporate into the nation all ethnic Germans, and violent nationalism. Anti-Semitism also suggests that the strain centered on the economic and occupational aspects of the societal community; the Jew symbolized a dangerous and unscrupulous competitor who could not be trusted because he did not "belong" in the national ethnic community. Indeed, the emphasis on the virtues of *Gemeinschaft* in German social thought since the nineteenth century has had similar implications.[20]

The Nazi movement, even with its immense mobilization of power, seems to have been an acute sociopolitical disturbance, but not a source of major future structural patterns,[21] though it may have contributed to the postwar integration of the German societal community.

Although the political integration of any large-scale and changing society is always partial, France and Germany seem to have experienced greater political instability both internally and externally than have others, especially those that we shall treat as "integrative" to the modern system. France has had three monarchical and five republican regimes since the Revolution. Germany's new democratic system, established after World

[19] See Rainer Baum, "Values and Uneven Political Development in Imperial Germany," unpublished doctoral dissertation, Harvard University, 1967.

[20] See Talcott Parsons, "Democracy and Social Structure in Pre-Nazi Germany," in *Essays in Sociological Theory* (rev. ed.; New York: Free Press, 1954). On the relations between anti-Semitism and anticommunism, see "Social Strains in America," in *Structure and Process in Modern Societies* (New York: Free Press, 1960); and "Full Citizenship for the Negro American?" in Talcott Parsons and Kenneth Clark (eds.), *The Negro American* (Boston: Houghton-Mifflin, 1966). The latter two essays are reprinted in *Politics and Social Structure* (New York: Free Press, 1969).

[21] The contrary interpretation has been presented in a great many works of social criticism over the past thirty years. A few leading examples are Erich Fromm, *Escape From Freedom* (New York: Holt, 1941); Hannah Arendt, *The Origins of Totalitarianism* (2nd ed.; New York: Meridian, 1958); and Erich Voegelin, *The New Science of Politics* (Chicago: University of Chicago Press, 1952). A particularly interesting treatment of this problem is contained in Barrington Moore, Jr., *Social Origins of Dictatorship and Democracy* (Boston: Beacon, 1966).

130

War I, gave way to Nazism in only fifteen years. Even aside from its partition, its present stability is somewhat precarious, though a direct revival of Nazism seems unlikely.

Franco-German relations were central to the international disturbances that set off the two world wars. The European-unification movement, though it has encountered serious obstacles since De Gaulle's accession to power, may help to stabilize the situation, especially with its economic base in the Common Market. The survival of the United Nations for more than twenty years and the moderate easing of East-West tensions may encourage such stabilization.

The special status of "intellectuals" is important, particularly in France [22] but also in Germany and Italy. These countries are perhaps the central focus of the great heritage of European intellectual culture. Historically, this heritage has been closely associated with both aristocracy and the Church, and the decline of these institutions has contributed to the intellectuals' prominence.

In contrast to that in the United States, the European academic world has tended much less toward professionalism, having absorbed fewer of the primary intellectual functions, e.g. concentrating on humanistic "writing." Intellectuals are a less differentiated group, despite their older traditions. The more strictly intellectual disciplines are more closely connected with the arts—"Bohemian" society constitutes a kind of emancipated élite, sharing with the aristocracy a contempt for things "bourgeois." Their special concern with highly generalized culture is one principal reason for treating France and Germany as the core of the pattern-maintenance system of modern European societies, despite their political instability.

The old "southern tier" has become relatively weak. Spain became isolated, involved in internal difficulties, and the first of the great colonial powers to lose the bulk of its empire. The rise of Bismarckian Germany weakened the Austrian empire, which collapsed after World War I. Italy was unified a century ago but did not emerge as a first-class power.

The northwest corner of the old European system—now comprising Great Britain, Holland, and Scandinavia but not France— is primarily "integrative" for the modern system. Belgium might also be included, despite the severity of its internal ethnic-linguistic division, as might Switzerland.[23] The integrative societies have mature and relatively stable

---

[22] See Michel Crozier, "The Cultural Revolution: Notes on the Changes in the Intellectual Climate in France," in Graubard, op. cit.

[23] Canada and Australia might also be included in the "integrative" category. See S. M. Lipset on their differences from the United States in The First New Nation (New York: Basic Books, 1965). Today's Austria seems to belong more to the pattern-maintenance group, however.

democratic political institutions and well-organized party systems.[24] The Fascist movements did not make great headway in these countries.

Although the line between the civil-law and common-law traditions runs through this cluster of societies, all have solid legal systems relatively independent of political pressures. All have strong traditions of civil liberties, and in none has the complex of laws governing property and contract been seriously undermined by radical socialist policies. All except Belgium now enjoy relative ethnic and linguistic homogeneity.

These societies also have highly developed "welfare states," in which social insurance and other redistributive benefits enhance social security, especially for lower-income groups. This development has been supported by the democratic-socialist parties, which have generally separated themselves from the communist movement and gained widespread support, often majorities. The impact of socialism has been more important in welfare policies than in socialization of the means of production.

Social and cultural developments in these countries reflect comparative affluence and are based on strong industrial economies in Britain and Sweden and a more commercial one in Holland. Compared with those of Germany and the United States, Britain's economic-growth rate slowed markedly in the late nineteenth century, and its heavy dependence upon foreign trade and the changes in its world political position have since caused further difficulties. Probably the British economy will soon be incorporated into the European Common Market.

The stratification patterns of the integrative societies are in one sense of an intermediate type. In terms of *relative* welfare, the integrative societies have aided and supported their lower-income and -status groups to degrees exceeding all but the outright socialist societies. In contrast to American and Soviet societies, they have continued to permit aristocratic elements to share in defining the "establishments," especially in Great Britain. Liberalization of opportunities for social mobility—especially the British Education Act of 1944—have taken the place of the kind of broad status differentiation and mass educational upgrading so conspicuous in the United States.[25] Nevertheless, the stratification pattern has probably begun to shift in the direction of the model. Sweden has also retained some aspects of aristocracy, somewhat resembling those of Germany.

Throughout the modern system, the main trend has been for "class" status to become focused on one broad central category—which, however,

---

[24] See the relevant contributions in S. M. Lipset and S. Rokkan (eds.), *Cleavage Structures, Party Systems, and Voter Alignment* (New York: Free Press, 1967); and in Robert Dahl (ed.), *Political Oppositions in Western Democracies* (New Haven: Yale University Press, 1966).
    [25] See T. H. Marshall, *Class, Citizenship and Social Development* (New York, Anchor, 1965).

132

must be reconciled with differential income, various life styles and symbols, and inequalities in political power. The American stratification system is focused on the middle class. The position of an "upper class" is relatively unpopular and tenuous. Where it has survived, it has been more as a "power élite." Furthermore, there are now few working-class people in the classical sense, only the "poor." In the Soviet Union all respectable people, including industrial managers, scientists, government administrators, and assorted intellectuals (the "intelligentsia") are considered members of the "working class." The other two main sectors of the modern system have preserved more elements of the traditional "capitalist" two-class system, though in varying guises. Class and status conditions are rapidly changing in character practically everywhere in the modern system, however.

Although the industrial and democratic revolutions are still vital forces in the new Europe, probably the most important development is the educational revolution. In an important sense, its groundwork was laid in the old Europe, in the cultural tradition and in establishment of universal public education for the first time in large-scale societies, especially in Germany; England lagged in this respect.[26] Compared to the United States and the Soviet Union, the pattern-maintenance and integrative societies have been "conservative" in regard to the educational revolution but are now moving into it. This trend will promote the growth of "meritocracy" and pose the problem of balancing technical competence and "humanistic cultivation" in higher education. The great humanstic traditions of the leading European countries will become part of the cultural underpinnings of all modern "educated" classes. Such "infusions" will probably modify the biasses of current cultural "Americanism."

Student unrest has emerged practically everywhere in the modern system, in both socialist and capitalist societies.[27] It involves the relations between the democratic and educational revolutions, as well as certain consequences of the industrial revolution—for example, the economic capacity to support mass higher education and sufficient demand for people with higher education in the occupational system.

The question of student status within the academic system is rela-

26 David Landes, "Technological Change and Development in Western Europe, 1750–1914," in H. J. Habakkuk and M. Postan (eds.), *The Industrial Revolutions and After* (Cambridge, Eng.: Cambridge University Press, 1965), vol. 6 of *The Cambridge Economic History of Europe.*

27 Student unrest and activism have also been very conspicuous in a range of societies that we would classify as "modernizing," rather than modern. The earliest wave seems to have been in Latin America, but other waves have become prominent, for example, in India and in Indonesia. How the "Red Guard" movement in China fits into this framework is questionable. At any rate, our comments are directed only at the generality of this phenomenon in societies that are relatively modern by our criteria.

133

tively unsettled, and there are striking parallels between the student movements of today and the labor movements of the nineteenth century. Within the academic system students occupy the lowest positions in prestige and authority. Furthermore, many students' parents have not had higher education,[28] a parallel to industrial workers who migrated from the rural areas. Both movements have been characterized by democratic ideologies with strong utopian strains; the extreme student position is a demand for fully democratic government of universities so that any student would become the equal of a senior professor. This movement already seems to be splitting into a radical and a moderate wing, as did the labor movement. Furthermore, student activism, like labor activism, has two possible focal points: the academic system itself and public policy generally.

The parallel has limits, of course. The status of student, unlike that of worker, is temporary. Furthermore, the distinction between workers and "capitalists" was based on inherited class position, whereas that between faculty and administration on one side and students on the other is not. At any rate, student unrest is clearly connected with the new level of mass higher education.

Modernization of Non-Western Societies

Both the United States and Soviet Russia have basically European cultural traditions and have interacted closely with Europe for centuries. The modern system has extended beyond the "Western" cultural areas, however.[29] Since the fifteenth and sixteenth centuries European influence has pervaded virtually all the rest of the world through trade, missions, settlements, and acquisition as colonies.

Japan, however, became moderized without European culture or population. Japan's two and one-half centuries of self-imposed isolation from both the West and mainland Asia under the Tokugawa regime was largely defensive, as were its first steps toward modernization, following the recognition that continued isolation was impossible. The country first adopted a modernizing pattern closer to that of the eastern wing of the European system than to that of the British-American wing. Imperial Meiji Japan modeled its constitution after that of imperial Germany,[30]

[28] Martin Meyerson, "The Ethos of the American College Student," *Daedalus* (Summer 1966), 713–39.

[29] A more extensive general introduction to this question from a point of view similar to that outlined here is S. N. Eisenstadt, *Modernization: Protest and Change* (Englewood Cliffs, N.J.: Prentice-Hall, 1966).

[30] See Reinhard Bendix, *Nation-Building and Citizenship* (New York: Wiley, 1964).

new counterpoints

granting special constitutional privileges to the military forces and establishing a centralized national educational system. Also the regime tolerated, though it did not directly further, the concentration of economic power in the *zaibatsu* firms.

The selective borrowing of East European institutional patterns fitted Japan neatly. Tokugawa social structure generally emphasized collective goal attainment.[31] Although in certain respects it was "feudally" decentralized, its organization was hierarchical and its human resources easily mobilized, both in the daimyos' territorial domains and in their lineal kinship structure.

Japan thus had at least the potential for an integrated political system, which, after the Meiji "revolution," was able to give central direction to modernization. Comparable institutional resources did not exist in, for example, China or India.[32] Furthermore, in relation to an Asian "frontier" and the exigencies of rapid development, Japan was comparable to Prussia and later the Soviet Union, where central governmental authority has also been very important. The Tokugawa regime seems to have been oriented primarily toward keeping its "feudal" units in a static balance, which, however, rendered certain internal structures precarious. The Meiji Restoration, oriented toward foreign relations, mobilized these units nationally.

Despite the "fit" between Japan's indigenous and borrowed elements, modernization occasioned severe strains, especially in developing formally patrimonial bureaucratic organization in government and business. These strains were probably the primary source of Japan's post-World War I tendency toward Fascism, which somewhat paralleled German developments in that period.[33] Despite important differences between the two societies, parliamentarianism and related structures in Japan and their German counterparts were subject to similar heavy pressures. Also both nations, encouraged by "power vacuums," embarked on militaristic expansion policies.

After Japan's alignment with the Axis powers in World War II, its defeat precipitated another major turning point. Under American occupation and as an American ally Japan has repudiated its immediate semi-Fascist past and has developed a democratic parliamentary regime. Despite a strong internal socialist-communist movement, it has generally supported the "free" democratic nations in the cold war. There has been further industrialization and modernization, including a break in population

---

[31] See Robert N. Bellah, *Tokugawa Religion* (New York: Free Press, 1957).
[32] See Talcott Parsons, *Societies: Evolutionary and Comparative Perspectives* (Englewood Cliffs, N.J.: Prentice-Hall, 1966) and references cited there.
[33] Masau Maruyama, *Thought and Behavior in Modern Japanese Politics* (London: Oxford University Press, 1963).

growth. Japanese agriculture has modernized around a family farm system, making collectivization unnecessary, a feature that Japan shares with the United States, Great Britain, and, increasingly, Western Europe.

Despite Japan's well-advanced modernization, its particular patterns are difficult to assess. Indeed, it seems that Japan has not yet "shaken down" to stability. Its early leanings toward the Prussian model were grounded in its indigenous social structure, but they were also nurtured by an international environment in which aggressive defensiveness and then national expansionism "paid off." Since 1945 Japan has turned sharply toward an adaptive-integrative pattern. Japan's future course, more than that of most industrial societies, will probably depend upon its world position, notably upon whether or not it is drawn into Communist China's increasingly powerful orbit. A liberal adaptive-integrative pattern may become firmly institutionalized in Japan, but it need not closely approximate the American pattern, especially at two points.

First, the pattern of political legitimation, symbolized by the imperial institution, has inherent instabilities. Unlike the top authority structures of other modern societies, that of Japan is not directly grounded in one of the great historic religions, Christianity, Confucianism, or Buddhism or in one of their derivatives like Marxism. It rests on an historic-ethnic basis with no inherent generalized orientation from which a probable societal tendency can be firmly predicted.[34] The consequences for Japan of the rationalizing pressures of modernity are uncertain, though it may develop a constitutional monarchy of the British-Scandinavian type. Second, Japan has no strongly institutionalized legal system in the Western sense.[35] Even recently Japan's legal institutions seem weaker than those of pre-revolutionary Russia, for example. The severe conflicts of interest inherent in rapid modernization must correspondingly be contained largely by political processes rather than by formal adjudication and by attendant informal adjustments somewhat independent of politics. The political process must therefore carry an unusually heavy burden of integration in Japan.

These considerations suggest that Japan has less built-in stability than have several other modern societies. Yet the nation has certainly traveled far along the paths of industrial, democratic, and educational revolution and is the first major example of relatively full modernization of a large and totally non-Western society. Its developmental experience

[34] See S. N. Eisenstadt, "The McIver Lecture: Transformation of Social, Political, and Cultural Orders in Modernization," *American Sociological Review*, 30 (October 1965), 659–73.
[35] Richard William Rabinowitz, "The Japanese Lawyer," unpublished doctoral dissertation, Harvard University, 1956).

136

thus raises some very broad questions about the future of the system of modernized and modernizing societies.

The "imperialist" phase of Western society's relations with the rest of the world was transitional. The trend toward modernization has now become worldwide. In particular, the élites of most nonmodern societies accept crucial aspects of the values of modernity, especially economic development, education, political independence, and some form of "democracy." Though the institutionalization of these values is—and will long remain—uneven and fraught with conflict, the trend toward modernization in the non-Western world will probably continue. We cannot expect a clear outcome of the contemporary post-imperialist ferment for a considerable time. But the burden of proof rests with those who argue that any major part of the world will settle into a clearly *non*modern pattern of society during the next couple of centuries, though the variations within the modern type of society will probably turn out to be very great.

The prospects for successful modernization of such societies are so complex a question and have been dealt with by so many social scientists that it seems best to limit ourselves to only two points here. First, the decline of the colonial empires, combined with the cold war division within the modern system, has created a climate for the emergence of a "third world" bloc as a stabilizing factor in the world and in the spread of modernism. It can become a classic example of *tertius gaudens*. Second, to the extent that Japan achieves successful modernization and stability as a predominantly integrative society, it may rise to a position of the first importance as a model for modernizing non-Western societies and as a factor in the balance of international power.

conclusion:
the main pattern
eight

A complex problem of perspective is involved when, as in this volume a study covers a time span of several centuries ending with the discussion of quite contemporary issues in the societies in which both the author and most of his readers are participants. This problem is especially apparent in our treatment of conflict and strain in the latter part of Chapter 6 and discussion of the rationale for emphasizing American society at the beginning of Chapter 7. In these discussions, more conspicuously than in the rest of the book, the difficulty of objectivity in the selection of problems and phenomena from the welter of contemporary issues and available information becomes acute, particularly because not only is there considerable variation of opinion within the relevant branches of social science but also many of these differences shade into those that should properly be called "ideological."

The best strategy for maintaining objectivity thus lies in emphasis upon the *match* between the theoretical scheme employed in the study, which is explicitly comparative and evolutionary, and the statements of empirical fact that have been selected to validate theoretical interpretation. It is, of course, important to keep in mind that this volume and its

138

companion [1] have been conceived together. The longer the time span and the wider the comparative range within which such an analytical scheme is put to empirical test, the likelier it is that the salient empirical features and developmental trends that emerge are both empirically valid and theoretically significant.

This perspective appears to be very much in the spirit of Weber's views both of the general nature of sociocultural evolution and of the nature of modern society. The reader familiar with Weber's work will, however, be aware that this book is not simply an attempt to "bring Weber up to date" but also involves substantial differences in emphasis in the interpretation of structures and trends. How far Weber would have adhered to these differences, had he lived to experience the intervening half-century of social events and scientific development, we naturally cannot know. We agree entirely with Weber, however, in his judgment that the development of what he called Western society in the modern era is of "universal" significance in human history and in the corollary of that judgment: that the development has not been random but definitely *directional.*

This directionality is one aspect of a threefold conception of the ways in which modern societies constitute a single system. A second is the thesis that the modern type has had a single origin, which was discussed at some length in the "Introduction" and was put forth by Weber. The third aspect, the sense in which the modern system has been a differentiated system of (several) societies requires elucidation, however.

In Chapter 3 we stressed that already in feudal times the European system was differentiated internally along functional lines. This differentiation was much advanced by the seventeenth century and, along with the extension of the system beyond its original geographical boundaries, has persisted into our own time. From one point of view later developments in this direction—the division between predominantly Roman Catholic and Protestant areas and among ethnically and linguistically distinctive "nations" and politically independent states—involved "disintegration" of the medieval unity of Western Christendom under the Church and the Holy Roman Empire. The process was not simply one of disintegration, however; it also had positive significance for the system as a whole. Such differentiation was a major contribution to the capacity of the system not only to initiate but also to create the conditions for institutionalization of significant evolutionary change. Despite fragmentation "the West" . was, throughout the period of our concern, an area with a common culture

[1] Talcott Parsons, *Societies: Evolutionary and Comparative Perspectives* (Englewood Cliffs, N.J.: Prentice-Hall, 1966).

based on the Christian religious tradition and its heritage from the Israel and Greece of classical antiquity; the latter assumed independent significance through both the Roman institutional heritage and its re-emergence in the Renaissance. It is because of our conviction of the importance of this common heritage that we devoted so much space to it in Chapter 3.

Within this common framework, which included an only very partially and precariously institutionalized political order, the kinds of innovation that we have emphasized had a certain "resonance" in parts of the system other than those in which they mainly occurred. English common law thus could be linked with the revived traditions of Roman law in England's own heritage and on the Continent and with the traditions of Protestantism—after all Calvin was a Frenchman and Luther a German. The British gentry could be linked with more general patterns of aristocracy, and the economic development of England and Holland was continuous with that of northern Italy and the free-city belt along the Rhine. Culturally the links between Italian science represented by Galileo and English science represented by Newton were crucial, as were those in philosophy, as between the French Descartes, the English Hobbes and Locke, the German Leibniz.

In the last chapter we spoke of the "Americanization" of Western Europe in the present century, which is another example of this kind of interplay. The American heritage is, of course, basically European, though in selective and modified form. But the United States has remained part of the same system as Europe and in turn has influenced the rest of it.

There has, of course, been a great deal of conflict, "frontier" primitivism, and lag in some of the older parts of the system relative to the more progressive parts. Some aspects of the Counter-Reformation offer an example, as do some aspects of British and French "backwardness" in industrial organization relative to the United States. Conversely, until the present generation many cultivated Europeans regarded the United States as a kind of culturally crude frontier society.[2]

These strains and conflicts are apparent both within particular societies and in intersocietal relations, and here may be an appropriate place to say a little about the latter. There are two general reasons why manifestations of strains and underlying conflicts should be more salient in intergroup than in intragroup relations. One is that solidarity is stronger within a group—including a "national" societal community—than

---

[2] To give a personal example, when I was a student in Germany more than forty years ago, I was asked by a young lady at a dance why I had chosen to study in Germany. On replying that I was concerned to learn something about German (academic) culture, she replied that she understood, as "Bei Ihnen gibt es wohl keine Wissenschaft," a view that even then I resented but that could hardly be seriously defended today.

conclusion: the main pattern

between it and others of its type, and therefore there is a tendency to "displace" conflict into the field of intergroup relations. Second, almost by definition, intergroup order is less firmly institutionalized than is intragroup order at corresponding levels, for defenses against the cycles of escalating conflict are weaker. In the international sphere, of course, the tendency is for this escalation to culminate in wars, for control of organized force is weakest at that point, and organized force is the ultimate coercive instrument. Certainly the history of modern societal systems has been one of frequent, if not continual, warfare. Although the system of modern societies, includes certain self-limiting factors—or rather, built-in mitigating factors— with respect to conflict, on several occasions wars have been highly destructive, perhaps most notably in the wars of religion of the sixteenth and seventeenth centuries, the wars of the French Revolution and the Napoleonic period, and the two great world wars of the twentieth century; the succeeding period is under the still greater threat of nuclear war. The striking point is that the *same* system of societies within which the evolutionary process that we have traced has occurred has been subject to a high incident of violence, most conspicuously in war but also internally, including revolutions.

These facts are not incompatible with what seems a secular trend toward reduction of violence both internally and internationally.[3] Current widespread fears of imminent and ultimate nuclear holocaust raise a question that cannot be answered objectively with much confidence. Our view is relatively optimistic:that there is sufficient motivation on the side of societal responsibility to make retreat from actual total conflict, as in the Cuban missile crisis of 1962, probable.

One more point may be made. A further indication of the importance of the *system* of societies is that the most serious conflicts seem to occur between those units that have the most widely differing roles and values within the system. Clearly the Reformation and its aftermath introduced a major fissure in the European system—extending to a serious disturbance of Franco-British relations over the status of the Stuart dynasty. At the same time both the Roman Catholic and Protestant "camps" were clearly part of Western Christendom. The disturbances following the French Revolution were in some respects similar, as indeed are those of the cold-war period that still continues. Marxism—even as it operates in China— is thus as much a part of the Western cultural heritage as was Protestantism in an earlier period. This type of conflict clearly is not proof that a

[3] See Talcott Parsons, "Order as a Sociological Problem," in Paul G. Kuntz (ed.), *The Concept of Order* (Seattle: University of Washington Press, 1968); and Parsons, "Some Reflections on the Place of Force in Social Process," in Harry Eckstein (ed.), *Internal War: Basic Problems and Approaches* (New York: Free Press, 1964), reprinted in Parsons, *Sociological Theory and Modern Society*.

modern "system" in our sense does not exist.[4] Widespread pessimism over the survival of modern society is closely linked to doubts, especially among intellectuals, about the actual viability of modern societies and their moral right to survive without the most radical changes. Indeed it is often alleged that modern society is "totally corrupt," can be cleansed only by total revolution, and is ripe for it.

Our grounds for skepticism about this position have been stated at the end of Chapter 6. The very substantial increment of value institutionalization that has in fact occurred in the last century, for example, is difficult to reconcile with the diagnosis of nearly total corruption; though alienation is, of course, both intense and widespread in important groups, the structural prerequisites for a major revolution are difficult to discern. For example, it is difficult to believe that structural injustices are nearly as great as those proclaimed as justification for the coming proletarian revolution by Marx and Engels just over a century ago in the *Communist Manifesto*. Yet, with the wisdom of hindsight, we cannot but be impressed that "the revolution," in this classic sense, has not occurred in a single industrially advanced country but has been confined to relatively "underdeveloped" societies—of which the Russia of 1917 was surely an example—and those under the military domination of such societies, as were Poland and Czechoslovakia after 1945.

The explanation of the prevalence and intensity of what we call "ideological pessimism" about modern societies clearly presents problems beyond the scope of this small book.[5] Our present concern is to establish sufficient doubt of the validity of such views so that the reader will not jump to the facile conclusion that the main trend of modern development over the past several centuries has suddenly come to an end and that therefore the perspective expressed in these two volumes is not relevant to assessment of the coming phases. It is our personal conviction that, though

[4] The conflicts involved in so-called "imperialism" are of a somewhat different character, generally associated with the emergence of greatly enhanced adaptive political capacity in some sectors of a system, which in turn leads to assumption of political control over less advanced units in areas of what is sometimes called "power vacuum." This political control is, however, generally rather incompletely institutionalized, and a shift of balance can then activate, or present opportunities for, "liberation" movements.

[5] Such pessimism is, of course, by no means new. The famous example of Christian pessimism about the society of the early Roman Empire, which was surely by comparative sociological standards not totally corrupt, may be cited, and a similar note became prevalent in the Reformation. An interesting and possibly suggestive comparison, however, is with Colonial New England, where, as Perry Miller describes it, under the stress of misfortune, whatever its source, a "jeremiad" often took place, a kind of orgy of guilty self-accusation by colonists, who insisted that *they* had failed to live up to their obligations on their "errand" into the wilderness. It suggests that a highly activist, this-worldly value pattern makes people especially sensitive to the gaps between expectation and performance; at the extreme they attribute *all* such gaps to the shortcomings of the current generation. See Perry Miller, *Nature's Nation* (Cambridge, Mass.: Harvard University Press, 1968).

142

conclusion: the main pattern

major changes are in process, the sociologist of the twenty-first century will discern just as many factors of continuity with the past as as we can now discern with the nineteenth century and, of course, those previous to it. This *conviction*, however, is not a *prediction*, which the critic could legitimately insist be stated more precisely or retracted.

Finally, let us repeat the final note of Chapter 6, the conviction that the present crisis—and there does seem to be one—centers in the societal community, not in the economy, the polity, or the value system. Compared even to the nineteenth century, there have been major changes in modern societal communities, especially in mutual adjustment to the impact of the industrial and the democratic revolutions. Much more recently the impact of the educational revolution has grown to the first importance. It is our conviction that the coming phase will center on integrating the consequences of all three of these major changes, both mutually and with the exigencies of the societal community. The most acute problems will presumably be in two areas. First is the development of the cultural system as such in relation to the society. We may picture it as focused on certain problems of "rationality," or of what Weber called the "process of rationalization." Second is the problem of the motivational bases of social solidarity within a large-scale and extensive society that has grown to be highly pluralistic in structure. We know that the cruder simplicities of the *Gemeinschaft* school of thought cannot be institutionalized, but we also know that some of the major problems lie in this *area*. Furthermore, neither set of problems will be "solved" without a great deal of conflict.

We should expect that anything like a "culminating" phase of modern development is a good way off—very likely a century or more. Talk of "postmodern" society is thus decidely premature.[6] Taking into account the undeniable possibility of overwhelming destruction, our expectation is nevertheless that the main trend of the next century or more will be toward completion of the type of society that we have called "modern."

[6] See John Porter, "The Future of Upward Mobility," *American Sociological Review*, 33, No. 1 (February 1968), 5–19.

selected references

In line with the continued concern with the framework of societal evolution, I should like to suggest first, reference to standard works on the status of biological evolution: Simpson, *The Meaning of Evolution* (New Haven: Yale University Press, 1950); Mayr, *Animal Species and Evolution* (Cambridge: Harvard University Press, 1963); and articles by Stern, "The Continuity of Genetics," Stent, "DNA," Olby, "Francis Crick, DNA, and the Central Dogma," and Pauling, "Fifty Years of Progress in Structural Chemistry and Molecular Biology," from *Daedalus* (fall, 1970).

The most important single reference for interpretation of modern society is the work of Max Weber, especially his introduction to the series of studies in the sociology of religion, an English translation of which is reprinted in my edition of *The Protestant Ethic and the Spirit of Capitalism* (New York: Scribner's, 1930). In the background of Weber's thinking, of course, lay that of Marx, most massively developed in *Das Kapital* (3 vols., F. Engels, ed., International Publishing Co.), and of Hegel, in his *Philosophy of History* (New York: Dover, 1956).

The theoretical orientation is, to a high degree, the author's own. Among a good many items which might be mentioned, let me first sight the *Theories of Society* (New York: Free Press, 1961), of which I was senior editor—including both the selections and the introductory materials, especially my own part in the

144

general introduction ("An Outline of the Social System," Talcott Parsons, pp. 30–79) and my Introduction to part four (pp. 963–93). An essay, "Evolutionary Universals in Society," which is included in the collection *Sociological Theory and Modern Society* (New York: Free Press, 1967), is particularly important, as is the article under the title "Christianity," in the *Encyclopedia of the Social Sciences* (8 vols., E. R. Seligman, ed.; New York: Macmillan). Another collection of essays under the title *Politics and Social Structure* (New York: Free Press, 1969), overlaps substantially with *Sociological Theory* (New York: Free Press, 1954), but has some additional relevant materials. Finally, an essay, "Equality and Inequality in Modern Society, or Social Stratification Revisited" for *Sociological Inquiry* is pertinent to the general theoretical perspective. [This issue of *Sociological Inquiry* is published by Bobbs-Merrill, under the title of *Social Stratification: Theory and Research* (Indianapolis: 1970).]

Among other contemporaries and near contemporaries, there are important debts to a variety of authors. Within a much longer list, let me simply mention Robert Merton, *Social Theory and Social Structure*, 3rd ed. (New York: Free Press); Neil Smelser, *Industrial Revolution* (Chicago: Chicago University Press, 1959) and *Sociology of Economic Life* (Englewood Cliffs, N. J.: Prentice-Hall, 1963); Robert Bellah, *Beyond Belief* (New York: Harper, 1970); and more specific work of Weber's, *Sociology of Law, Sociology of Religion* (Boston: Beacon, 1964), and other parts of *Economy and Society* (3 vols., Gunther Roth and Claus Wittich, eds., Bedminster). I consider law to be particularly important, and especially mention Lon L. Fuller, *The Morality of Law* (New Haven: Yale University Press, 1964) and *Anatomy of the Law* (New York: Mentor, pb, 1969). Political sociology, especially associated with the work of S. M. Lipset and Stein Rokkan, has been most important. Perhaps Lipset and Rokkan, (eds.,) *Party Systems and Voter Alignments* (New York: Free Press, 1967) and Lipset's, *First New Nation* (New York: Basic Books, 1963), are the best references.

On the historical background, three writings of the late Professor A. D. Nock, *Conversion: the Old and the New in Religion from Alexander the Great to Augustine of Hippo* (New York: Oxford University Press, 1933), *St. Paul* (New York: Harper, 1968), and *Early Gentile Christianity* (New York: Harper, 1964) are particularly relevant. Also, Adolph von Harnack's, *Mission and Expansion* (New York: Harper, 1961); Werner Jaeger's *Early Christianity* (New York: Oxford University Press, 1969); Troeltsch's *Social Teachings in the Christian Churches* (New York: Harper, 1960); and Lietzman's *A History of the Early Church* (New York: Meridian World Publishing Co., 1961) are highly relevant. On the classical institutional heritage, Troeltsch, Lot, Henri Pirenne, C. H. McIlwain, Gierke, and Max Weber's *City* (New York: Free Press) are particularly important.

On the medieval society, the great source is Marc Bloch, *Feudal Society* (Chicago: Chicago University Press, 1968). However, Troeltsch is also highly relevant, as are Southern, *The Making of the Middle Ages* (New York: Yale University Press, pb, 1953), and on an especially important point, H. C. Lea, *History of Sacerdotal Celibacy* (New York: University Books, 1966). Literature on the Renaissance and Reformation is enormous. I should like to suggest J. H. Plumb, *The Renaissance* (New York: Harper, pb); Joseph Ben-David, *Sociology of Science* (Englewood Cliffs, N. J.: Prentice-Hall, 1971); and Paul O. Kristeller, *Renaissance Thought* (New York: Harper, pb). On certain aspects of the Reformation, besides Weber's *Protestant Ethic and the Spirit of Capitalism* (New York: Scribner, 1930), and the volume on the topic with a valuable introduction by S. N. Eisenstadt, *Max*

Weber: On Charisma and Institution Building (Chicago: University of Chicago Press, 1968), I would like to mention two particularly important sources, namely Erik H. Erikson's *Young Man Luther* (New York: Norton, 1958), and David Little's *Religion, Order and Law* (New York: Harper, 1970). Of a similar special significance is Benjamin Nelson, *The Idea of Usury*, 2nd ed. (Chicago: University of Chicago Press, 1969).

For the general setting, a still very valuable source is Lord Bryce's *The Holy Roman Empire* (New York: Schocken Books, 1961), and on the religious side, of course, Troeltsch's *Social Teachings* (op. cit.). A monumental survey of the religious problem in England is given by W. K. Jordan in *The Development of Religious Toleration in England* (5 vols., Cambridge: Harvard University Press, 1932–1940). On the political side, see Max Beloff's *The Age of Absolutism* (New York: Harper, pb), and Barrington Moore's *Social Origins of Dictatorship and Democracy* (Boston: Beacon Press, 1966). On the earlier origins of parliament, C. H. McIlwain, *The High Court of Parliament* (New Haven: Yale University Press, 1910) and Namier are very valuable. Also, T. H. Marshall's *Class, Citizenship and Social Development* (New York: Doubleday, Anchor pb, 1964); Merton's classical essay on *Science, Technology and Society in Seventeenth Century England* (New York: Harper, 1970); and Tawney's *Religion and the Rise of Capitalism* (New York: Mentor, pb) should also be consulted.

For somewhat later developments, on the political side, much the most comprehensive source is R. R. Palmer's *The Age of the Democratic Revolution* (Princeton, N. J.: Princeton University Press, 1969). Michael Polanyi's *The Great Transformation* (Boston: Beacon Press, 1944) is also very illuminating. And with respect to the general sweep of the Industrial Revolution, see not only Clapham's *The Economic Development*

145

of France and Germany, 4th ed. (New York: Cambridge University Press, pb, 1935), but also David Landes, Unbound Prometheus (New York: Cambridge University Press, pb). On the background of political thought, J. W. Allen's A History of Political Thought in the 16th Century (New York: Barnes & Noble, 1960) should be consulted. For the social psychology of the development of the Democratic Revolution, see F. Weinstein and G. M. Platt, Wish to Be Free: Society, Psyche, and Value Change (Berkeley and Los Angeles: University of California Press, 1969).

Turning to the American case, Toqueville's Democracy in America (New York: Vintage, pb) continues to be a major reference point. Various works of Perry Miller are particularly important for the cultural background, notably Errand into the Wilderness (New York: Harper, pb) and for the transition into the 19th century, Life of the Mind in America (New York: Harcourt, Brace & Jovanovich, 1965). Lipset's First New Nation (op. cit.) is also valuable. On specifically religious development, J. J. Loubser's Development of Religious Freedom (Cambridge: Harvard University Press, 1964, Ph.D. Dissertation). Beyond this, the literature becomes almost unmanageably diverse and prolific. To name a rather diverse list, Oscar Handlin, The Uprooted (Boston: Little-Brown, 1951); Clinton Rossiter, Seedtime of the Republic (New World, 1953); Hartz, The Liberal Tradition in America, an Interpretation of American Political Thought since the Revolution (New York: Harcourt, Brace & Jovanovich, 1955), various works of V. O. Key and Richard Hof-

stadter, Berle and Means, The Modern Corporation and Private Property (revised edition, New York: Harcourt, Brace & Jovanovich, Inc.); Allen, The Big Change, America Transforms Itself (New York: Harper, pb, 1969); Andre Siegfried's America Comes of Age (New York: Harcourt, Brace & Jovanovich, 1927); and of course Myrdal's An American Dilemma (New York: Harper, 1962).

For the latter phase of modernization in continental Europe and other areas, one might suggest, for the Soviet Union, Cyril Black, ed., Transformation of Russian Society: Aspects of Social Change since 1861 (Cambridge: Harvard University Press, 1960); Alex Inkeles and Raymond A. Bauer, The Soviet Citizen (Cambridge: Harvard University Press, 1959); Gregory Grossman, Economic Systems (Englewood Cliffs, N. J.: Prentice-Hall, 1967); Merle Fainsod, How Russia is Ruled, rev. ed. (Cambridge: Harvard University Press, 1963); Harold Berman, Justice in USSR: an Interpretation of Soviet Law (Cambridge: Harvard University Press, 1963); Robert Bellah, Tokugawa Religion (Boston: Beacon Press, 1970); Maruyama, Thought and Behavior in Modern Japanese Politics (New York: Oxford University Press, 1963); New Europe, Stephen R. Graubard, ed. (Boston: Beacon); and In Search of France S. H. Hoffmann et al., eds. (Boston: Harvard University Press).

Any such listing is woefully incomplete and is meant to be suggestive to the reader and to record to some extent works on which the author's opinions have been importantly dependent.

selected references

index

Absolutism: rejected, 91, 96, 127; as solution, 54, 56–57, 79
Accountability: bureaucratic, 104–5; institutionalization of, 120
Action systems: social systems as constituents of, 4–8
Adaptation: economy as subsystem of, 10–11; in modern systems, 123; as primary function of action system, 4–6; primacy of role and, 7 (see also Roles)
Adaptive capacity: of modern society, 3; Reformation and societal, 74
Adaptive upgrading: defined, 11, 26, 27; in 17th cen., 69
Agriculture: commercial (17th cen.), 64–66, 68; decline in independent proprietorship in, 110; family farm system of, 136; feudal, 38; market system and, 75; Prussian, 73
Alienation: from secular society, 31–34; societal self-sufficiency and, 9; value generalization and intellectual, 100; widespread, 142
American Protestantism, 49, 87–92
American Revolution, 90
Americanization, 129, 140
Anticlericalism: French, 56, 59; Russian, 56, 124
Aristocracy, 57–75: bourgeoisie and, 44–45, 59, 60, 81, 129; civil service and, 103–4; in commercial farming, 64–66, 68, 73; elimination of Russian, 124; feudal, 38, 41–45, 57–60, 111; French Revolution and privileges of, 79–81; functional equivalent to, in democracies, 102; gentry and, 60–61, 64–66, 140; holdover, 86, 131, 132; intellectual culture and, 131; lack of U.S., 90–91; legitimate hereditary status of, 37; urban, 39, 41–42
Aristotle, 45
Arts: foundations of modern, 15, 45–47, 99
Associational system: bureaucracy as collegial, 105–6; collegial, defined, 98; corporate, 25, 26, 103; decentralization of power in, 116; defined, 24–26; early Church as, 30, 31; intracommunity pluralism and institutionalization of, 103; leadership in, 102–4; legitimation of, 15; membership in, 24, 104; of towns, 39; U.S. societal community as, 92; valued, 15; (see also Bindingness; Voluntary association)
Augustine, St., 32, 33
Australia, 122
Austria, 50–53, 131: German uni-

Austria (Cont.):
fication and, 73; religious pluralism in, 72
Authoritarian state, 84
Authoritarianism, U.S. fear of, 93
Authoritative interpretation of normative order, 16
Authority: corporate legitimation and, 79; of monarch, 79; office holding and limits on, 91; political, 55, 80–81; power and, 17; (see also Executive authority; Leadership)

Banking system, 76, 107
Behavioral organisms: as adaptive subsystems, 5; defined, 4, 6–7; primary zone of interpenetration for, 9
Belgium, 89, 131, 132
Bill of Rights (U.S.), 82, 94, 119
Bindingness: in electoral process, 82–83; as essential, 15–16, 24; in legal system, 18; of power, 17
Biological theory: continuity of society, culture and, 2
Bismarck, Otto von, 73
Bloch, 122
Bohemia, 51, 53
Botticelli, 46
Bourgeoisie, 39–46, 59–70: aristocracy and, 44–45, 59, 60, 81, 129; consolidation of, 44–45; corporate control by U.S., 104, 106; economic privileges of, 116; intellectual culture and, 131; mercantile and manufacturing, 66–67; ostentation and leisure of, 112–13; proletariat vs., 78, 115 (see also Two-class system; Working class); Russian, 124; as urban aristocracy, 39, 41–42
Bureaucracy: accountability and leadership by, 104–5; appointive office and, 103–4; "collegialized," 105–6; development of, 23–24, 87, 135; elective political office and, 102; of medieval Church, 34, 35; as negative symbol, 116–17; occupational roles in pattern of, 97–98
Byzantine Empire, 41

Calvin, John, 140
Calvinism: Prussian, 72–73; religious pluralism and, 55; South African, 100
Canada, 89, 122, 127
Canon law, 30, 40
Capitalism: bureaucratization of, 87; emergence of, 2, 3; family firm of early, 23; vs. socialism, 78, 96–97, 106–8, 111, 121; Renaissance and development of, 76; two-class system of early, 78; U.S. pattern of, distinctive, 107–8
Cathedrals, 39
Charlemagne, 34–35
Charles V, (Holy Roman Emperor), 50
China, 128, 135, 136, 141

Christ: as basis for religious collectivity, 31
Christian Church: as associational organization, 30, 31; legitimation by, 34–35; secular structure of, 38–40; (see also Roman Catholic Church)
Christianity: as cultural system, 29; early, 30–34; (see also Protestantism; Roman Catholicism)
Citizenship: as basis of inclusion in U.S. societal community, 92–94; development of, 21–22, 87; educational revolution and, 96, 97; elective office and, 102; in French Revolution, 80–84; Soviet, 125–27; universalistic criteria of U.S., 94; welfare minimum and, 110
City: as Christian symbol, 32; (see also Urban communities)
City-states, 41–42, 51, 52
Civil disobedience, morality legitimating, 19
Civil equality (see Egalitarianism)
Civil rights (see Citizenship; Equality of opportunity; Rights)
Civil service: aristocracy and, 103–4; (see also Bureaucracy)
Class conflict: concept of, 78; irrelevance of, 115–16
Class consciousness in U.S., 91
Classes: change in structure of modern, 113–14; leading, 113; of modern society, 112–13; main trend of, in modern system, 120, 132; U.S., 90–92; (see also Aristocracy; Bourgeoisie; Peasantry; Stratification system; Two-class system; Working class)
Coke, Sir Edward, 62
Collective representations: defined, 6, 9n
Collectivities: defined, 6–8; employment for membership in, 23, 24; (see also Membership)
Collegial association: bureaucracy as, 105–6; defined, 98
Colonial empires: decline of, 137
Commerce: growth of, 64; (see also Market system)
Commercial agriculture, 64–66, 68
Common law, 21, 62, 93, 140; origins of, 35
Common Market, 131, 132
Communism, 124, 125, 128; origins of, 2; secular anticlericalism in, 56
Communist parties, 100, 105; Russian, 125–27
Conflict: social, 140–43 (see also Class conflict)
Conservatism, Protestant, 49, 100
Conspicuous consumption, 113, 116
Constantine (Roman Emperor), 33
Constituency, 102 (see also Representative institutions)

147

Constitutional norms in legal system, 18–19
Constitutions: English, 68; U.S., 90, 92–94, 108
Consumer markets: occupational roles and extension of, 77
Consumer products: industrial revolution and, 75
Consumer sovereignty, 125
Consumption: conspicuous, 113, 116; of cultural goods, 112–13
Contract, market development and, 18, 22, 62, 63, 75, 79
Corporations: associational structure of, 25, 26, 103; development of private, 108; ownership and control of, 104, 106
Counter-Reformation, 51–52, 71, 80, 129, 140
Court systems: normative order and, 16
Cranach, Lucas, 47
Credit system: U.S., 107
Cromwell, Oliver, 57, 60
Cuban missile crisis (1962), 141
Cuius regio, eius religio formula, 51, 54–56, 58, 88, 128
Cultural goods: consumption of, 112–13
Cultural innovation: religious, 29, 46, 47 (see also Reformation); territorial state as, 42–43
Cultural system, 9–15: common European, delineated, 139–40; contemporary social structure and, 99; crisis in, 143; defined, 4, 5; differentiated, 15; legitimation of values and, 9–10, 13, 14; moral values in, 15; Reformation and, 47; of Renaissance, 45
Culture: as criterion of human society, 2, 3
Czechoslovakia, 128, 142

Darwinism, 99
Da Vinci, Leonardo, 46
Decision-making: associational, 25
Declaration of the Rights of Man, 82
De Gaulle, Charles, 131
Democratic institutions: dilemma of, 103
Democratic revolution, 79–85 (see also Citizenship; Egalitarianism): adjustment to, 143; educational revolution and, 96, 97; English, 79–81, 84; German, 130; Japanese, 136; in new Europe, 133; in Soviet Union, 124, 127
Democratic solidarity: institutionalization of, 25
Descartes, René, 142
Differentiation: in age of revolutions, 71–74; basic to modern philosophy, 46, 47; defined, 11, 26; in early Church, 30–32; of government, 16–17; hierarchy and social, 80; integration and societal, 18–26; in market system, 68–70; in medieval system, 35, 40–45, 57–59, 139–40; of polity and

Differentiation (Cont.): societal community, 101; in process of structural change, 26–28; production and, 87; Reformation, Counter-Reformation and, 51–52; in Renaissance, 45–47; in societal community, defined, 12–17
Division of labor: high degree of, in U.S., 91–92; in industrial revolution, 74, 77–78; medieval, 66; money, markets, and complex, 17, 27; social differentiations and, 80; for societal self-sufficiency, 8, 9
Dürer, Albrecht, 47
Durkheim, Emile, 6, 7, 74, 78

Economy, 64–75: command, of Soviet Union, 123–26; as primary societal subsystem, 10–11; retrogressive medieval, 38 (see also Feudalism); societal community and (defined) 17–18; (contemporary) 106–14; (17th cen.) 64–67; for societal self-sufficiency, 8–10; U.S., 91–92, 106–14; (see also Capitalism; Industrial revolution; Industrialization; Market system; Production)
Ecumenism, 99
Education: associational structure of higher, 26; development of secular, 88; of élite, 95; Soviet, 127–28
Education Act (British; 1944), 132
Educational revolution, 94–98; as crucial innovation, 114; equality and, 96, 97; institutionalization of intellectual disciplines by, 94–95, 99; in integrative societies, 133; non-familial roles in, 101; spread of, 22, 95, 132–36; student unrest and, 117–18, 133–34
Egalitarianism: in associations, 24; in early Church, 32; educational revolution and, 96, 97; in French Revolution, 80–82; generalization of, 118–21; in income distribution, 112; Protestant, 48; through franchise, 81–82, 84; in U.S., 94, 114–16; (see also Citizenship; Equality of opportunity; Rights)
Electoral process: accountability through, 105; bindingness in, 82–83; in collegial association, 105–6; (see also Franchise; Voting)
Eliot, T.S., 99
Empires: decline of colonial, 137; emergence of German, 73–74, 84–85
Empirical knowledge: as cultural system, 15
Employment: commitment of labor and conditions of, 17; for membership in collectivity, 23, 24; technological unemployment, 109–10

Enforcement: defined, 15–16; legitimate, 19
Engels, Frederick, 142
England: agriculture of, 64–66, 136; aristocracy of, 58–61, 64–65, 68, 81, 84; bourgeoisie of, 39–44, 60–66; civil service in, 104; democratic revolution in, 79–81, 84; economic development in, 64–70, 73–75, 76, 107, 123; educational revolution in, 132, 133; as integrative for modern system, 131–32; legal system of, 18, 62–64, 67, 68, 70, 108; religious pluralism in, 49, 51, 52, 55, 57, 88, 93; secularization of, 99; as territorial state, 42–43, 53, 54
England, Church of, 55
Environment: societal self-sufficiency and, 8–9
Equality (see Egalitarianism)
Equality of opportunity: capitalist competition guaranteeing, 111; educational revolution and, 95, 97; industrial revolution and, 81; institutionalization of, 120; socialist stress on, 114
Ethnicity: "Celtic," 57; egalitarianism undermining, 119; language and, 89–90; nationality and, 22; in U.S., 88–89, 92
Evolutionary change: process of, defined, 26–28
Executive authority: English, 60, 61; as collegial, 106; differentiation of, 19; of government, 16
Executive management, 25
Existentialism, 99–100

Family: contemporary occupational roles and isolation of, 100; farm system and, 136; labor in industrial revolution and, 77; as secure emotional base, 100–101; stratification and solidarity in, 96; in Soviet Union, 125
Fascism, 100, 129, 132, 135
Federalism: U.S., 93, 94, 102
Feudalism, 1–2; aristocracy under, 38, 41–45, 57–60, 111; as retrogressive, 36, 38; "subject" and, 21, 79, 87, 126; territorial state and, 42–43
Fiduciary: associational structure of boards, 25, 26, 103; roles in U.S., 108–9; subsystem, defined, 11
Financial markets, 76, 107
First Amendment (U.S. Constitution), 88
Flanders, 44, 47, 64
Ford, Henry, 107
France: as absolutist state, 57; aristocracy of, 58–61, 65–66, 79, 129; bourgeoisie of, 44, 59, 60, 129; civil service in, 104; democratic revolution in, 79; economic development of, 65, 74, 75; medieval, 41; as

148

index

France (Cont.):
pattern-maintenance base, 129; political instability of contemporary, 130–31; religious problem of, 56, 84; Roman Catholicism in, 50, 52; secularization of, 88, 99; as territorial state, 42–43, 53, 54
Franchise: in England, 55; formal power of, 102; political equality and, 82–83, 84; in Soviet Union, 126; universalization of, 21, 104
Fraternity (fraternité), 80, 83–84
Frederick the Great, 52
Free-enterprise system (see Capitalism)
French Revolution, 55, 117, 123, 129, 141: aristocratic privileges and, 79–81; citizenship as central concept in, 80–84; class splits fostering, 60; peasantry in, 65; secular anticlericalism in, 56, 59
Freud, Sigmund, 6
Fundamentalism: defined, 100

Galileo, 46, 47, 52, 140
Gaullism, 129
Gentry (English), 60–61, 64–66, 140
Geographic mobility, 100
Germany: democratic revolution in, 131; educational revolution in, 133; emergence of imperial, 73–74, 84–85; feudal, 42; industrial revolution in, 73–74, 107, 129–30; integration of, 123; investment banking system of, 76; as model for Japan, 134–35; national church in, 72; as pattern-maintenance base, 129; political instability of contemporary, 130–31; religious legitimacy in modern society and, 56; territorial states and, 52–54; white collar occupations in, 108; (see also Prussia)
Goal attainment: collectivities and primacy of, 7; defined, 4–6; by lead elements in modern system, 123; (see also Polity)
God: covenant with, 31; direct communion with, 47
Government: administration of, 23–24 (see also Bureaucracy); associationalism in, 24–25; differentiation of, defined, 16–17; franchise and system of, 82–83; free-enterprise and strong, 78; market system and, 22; separation of powers in U.S., 91–94; territorial jurisdiction and legitimation of, 20; (see also Legislative function; Monarchy; Parliamentary system; State, the)
Gratification: as primary goal of action, 5
Greece, 29–32, 140
Greek culture, 29–32, 140

Gregory VI (Pope), 39, 40
Guilds, 39, 44

Hapsburg dynasty, 50, 51, 53, 72
Hegel, Georg W.F., 1
Henry VIII, 49, 51
Hierarchy: abolishing, 119; of loyalties, 13; social differentiation and, 80
High-school dropouts, 95
Hobbes, Thomas, 12, 140
Hohenzollern dynasty, 72
Holbein, Hans, 47
Holland: 69, 75, 88; aristocracy of, 61, 65–66; democratic revolution in, 79; as integrative for modern system, 123, 131–32; market system in, 75; in power system (17th cen.), 54–56; religious pluralism in, 51, 52; Renaissance in, 47
Holy Roman Empire, 41, 42, 51–53
House of Commons, 61, 62, 67
House of Lords, 61, 63
Households: occupational roles and, 108, 109
Hungary, 50, 51, 53, 128

Ideological pessimism, 142
Immigrants: U.S., 87–90
Inclusion: citizenship as basis for, in U.S. society community, 92–94; of classical culture, 29–32, 45, 140; defined, 11, 26, 27; U.S. religious pluralism and process of, 88–89
Income: labor and money, 77; property, 111–12; salary and wage, 77, 110–11; U.S. distribution of, 110
India, 135
Individualistic social theory: self-interest in, 12-13
Individuals (see Personality system)
Industrial economy: social organization of productive process in, 22–23
Industrial revolution, 74–79: adjustment to, 117, 143; consumer products and, 75; differentiation by, 101; division of labor in, 74, 77–78; educational revolution and, 97; equality of opportunity and, 81; innovations in, 95–96; market economy and, 68–69; market system extended in, 75–79; primary economic organization of, 86; property and contract as essential to, 18, 22, 62, 63, 75, 79 (see also Proprietorship); spread of, 73–74, 107, 109
Industrialization, 124–36: of Germany, 129–30; of Japan, 135–36; of Soviet Union, 124, 125
Influence: in associations, 25; defined, 14, 121; money compared with, 27; power compared with, 17
Institutionalization: of accountability, 120; of associational

Institutionalization (Cont.):
organization, 103; of Church in Roman Empire, 33; of cultural systems, 10, 30; of intellectual disciplines, 94–95, 99; as interpenetration, 6; Reformation and, 48–49; of value patterns, 8, 9, 13
Integration: of contemporary social structure and cultural system, 99; defined, 4–6; Democratic revolution as, 75; educational revolution and, 133; function of norms in, 7; membership, 9; methods of, 18–26; in modern system, 123, 131–32, 136
Intellectual culture: aristocracy and, 131; development of, 46; institutionalization of, 94–95, 99
Intellectuals: status of French, 131; as suspicious, 71; value generalization and alienation of, 100
Interchange: process of, 6–7
Interest groups: U.S., 91
Intergroup relations, 140–41
Internalization: as interpenetration, 6
Interpenetration: zones of, defined, 6–7; roles and, 7
Intragroup relations, 140–41
Ireland, 57
Islam, 32
Israel, 29–33, 140
Italy, 129, 131: city-state organization of, 41–42, 51, 52; Counter-Reformation in, 71; Renaissance in, 45–47

James I (King of England), 62
Japan, 2; modernization of, 134–37
Jews, 88, 90, 130
John XXIII (Pope), 99
Judaism: Christianity and Palestinian, 30–33
Judicial review, 19, 20, 62, 93 (see also Legal system)
Junkers, 72–74, 132

Kant, Immanuel, 73
Kennedy, John F., 88
Khrushchev, Nikita S., 128
Kingship: territoriality and, 38, 58, 79; (see also Monarchy)
Kinship system: of American immigrants, 10; importance of, 11; in industrial revolution, 77; isolation of, 100; legitimation of, 40; in societal subsystems, 11; (see also Family)

Labor force: commitment of, 17; differentiated market developed from, 87; industrial revolution and, 77; mechanization and, 109–10; medieval hereditary, 38; women in, 101, 108; (see also Occupational roles; Working class)
Labor markets, 23, 24; upward spread of U.S., 108
Labor unions, 110–11

Labor-union movement: socialism and, 109; student movement compared with, 134
Land: as base for aristocracy, 38, 44, 57–60, 111; gentry, 60–61, 64–66, 140; proprietorship of, in U.S., 90
Language: ethnic membership and, 89–90
Law: defined, 18; Roman, 35, 62, 64, 140; (see also Legal system)
Leadership: in associational system, 102–4
Left: fundamentalism of extreme, 100
Legal profession: English, 62, 63; U.S., 93–94
Legal system, 18–20: Christian proselytization and Roman, 30; civil rights in, 82; continental, 62–64; English, 18, 62–64, 67, 68, 70, 108; industrial revolution and, 75, 78; of integrative countries in modern system, 132; Japanese, 136; of medieval Church, 35; Renaissance, 45–47; U.S., 18, 91, 93, 108; universalistic, 78, 86–87
Legislative function: defined, 16; legitimation of, 19–20
Legitimation: authority and corporate, 79; of associations, 15; Christ as, 31; by Church, 34–35; of feudalism, 36; heredity, 37 (see also Aristocracy); of kinship system, 40; of priesthood, 40, 48; of privilege, French Revolution and, 79–81; religious, of secular society, 52–56; of revolt, 18–19; of values, 9–10, 13, 14
Leo III (Pope), 35
Liberty (liberté), 80–81 (see also Egalitarianism)
Liege relationship, 38
Literacy, 95 (see also Educational revolution)
Locke, John, 69, 82
Loyalty: absolutism and, 56–57; defining obligations of, 12–13; feudal, 36–37
Luther, Martin, 48, 49, 140
Lutheranism, 72, 73

MacDonald, Dwight, 99
Machiavelli, Niccolò, 47
Magna Carta, 44
Majority rule: decision by vote and, 25 (see also Electoral process)
Management: control by, 108; of corporations, 104; occupationalizing, 112
Manor, 38
Market system: command economy and, 125–26; development of, defined, 22–24; disappearance of, 34; educational revolution and, 98; financial, 76, 107; industrial revolution and, 75–79; institutional foundations of differentiated, 68–70; normative order and, 17–18;

Market system (Cont.): occupational roles and, 77; production and differentiation through, 87; property, contract and, 18, 22, 62, 63, 75, 79; 17th cen. agricultural, 64, 65; towns and emerging, 44; U.S., 106
Marshall, T.H., 81, 93, 94
Marx, Karl, 1–2, 142
Mass production: development of, 107
Mechanization, 109
Medieval society, 35–45: differentiation in, 35, 40–45, 58–59, 139–40; division of labor in, 66; (see also Feudalism)
Membership: associational, 24, 104; defined, 20–22; equality of status in, 80–82; language and ethnic, 89–90; for societal self-sufficiency, 9; in U.S., on universalist grounds, 110; (see also Citizenship)
Merchant guilds, 44
Mexico, 107
Middle Ages (see Feudalism; Medieval society)
Milan, Edict of, 33
Military establishments: enforcements and, 15–16; Japanese, 135; medieval, 37–38; Prussian, 73
Mills, C. Wright, 116
Modern state: emergence of, 58, 84
Monarchy: abolition of Russian, 124; cuius regio, eius religo formula and, 51, 54–56, 58, 88, 128; development of, 42–45, 51; holdover, 84, 86; Junkers and, 73; power of French, 65; "subject" under, 21, 79, 87, 126; territoriality and, 38, 58, 79; (see also Absolutism; Aristocracy)
Monasticism, 33, 34, 47
Monetarization of economic affairs, 76, 107
Money: allocation and control of, 76; command economy and, 125–26; disappearance of, 34; influence compared with, 14; level of production and, 27; normative order and, 17–18; political integration and, 28
Monotheism: transcendental, 31
Moral legitimation of revolt, 18–19
Moral values: defined, 15 (see also Value systems)
Municipium, 36, 39

Naples and Sicily, Kingdom of, 50–51
Napoleon I, 84, 123
National churches, 49, 51, 54–55, 72
Nationalism, 84, 87, 92, 130: ethnic, 89; Gaullism and, 129; Hapsburg Empire and, 72; (see also Territoriality)
Nationality: basis for, 22
Nation-state: emergence of, 58, 67, 84 (see also State, the)

Naturalization, 93
Nazism, 129–31
Negroes, 91, 115; in inclusion process, 89, 94
New Left, 100, 117–18
Newton, Sir Isaac, 46, 69
Nominalism, 47
Normative order: as binding, 15–16; defined, 11–12; polity and, 18–20; (see also Legal system)
Norms: defined, 6–8; societal community and system of, 11–13
Nuclear war, 141

Occupational roles: consumer market extension and, 77; development of, in U.S., 87, 108–12; educational revolution and, 95, 97–98; isolation of family and, 100; spread of, 77–78
Office: appointive, 103–4; bureaucratic, defined, 23; elective, 91, 102; prestige of, 120–21; priesthood as, 34
Ortega y Gasset, José, 99
Orthodox Christianity, 41, 53, 124–25
Ownership (see Proprietorship)

Papacy: establishment of, 31–34; Italian city-states and, 51; states of, 41, 51; weakening of, 71, 129
Parlements, 59–60
Parliamentary system, 59–64; gentry and, 61; in Japan, 135; parlements compared with British, 59–60
Participation: as positive symbol, 117, 118; representative, 61
Participatory democracy, 117
Patriciates, 39, 41–42
Pattern maintenance: action system and, defined, 4–6, 98; cultural system and, 10–11; in English society, 67; Italy as principal base for, 42, 71; modern societal community and, 98–101; of "new" Europe, 129; societal community and, defined, 14–15; value primacy in, 7
Paul, St., 30
Peasantry: English, French and Dutch, 64–66; lack of U.S., 91
Personality system: Christian salvation and, 30, 31; defined, 4, 5; family and pattern maintenance of, 100—101; interpenetration in, 6–7; Protestantism and, 69–70; roles in, 7; "self-made man" as, 12–13, 96; for societal self-sufficiency, 9
Philosophy: importance of, 69, 99; modern, differentiation basic to, 46, 67; scholastic, 45–47
Physical environment: action systems and, 5; adaptive significance of, 8

Physical facilities: development of generalized, 77
Physical force: for societal self-sufficiency, 8
Physical resources: for societal self-sufficiency, 8, 10
Pluralism: religious, 21, 49–57, 67, 72, 86, 88–91, 93, 98–99; (see also Role-pluralism)
Pluralization: institutionalization and intracommunity, 103
Poland, 142
Police: enforcement and, 15–16
Political, the: concept of, 16
Political authority, 55, 80–81
Political leadership: accountability of, 104–5, 120; power of, 17; professional, 102; for societal self-sufficiency, 8–10; Soviet, as self-appointed, 126–27; territorial states and, 53, 54
Political parties: associationalism in, 25; European, 132; representative participation and, 61; U.S., 91, 102
Polity: as primary societal subsystem, defined, 10–11; (see also Economy)
Polity and societal community: contemporary, 101–6; defined, 15–17; differentiation of, 101; 17th cen., 50, 56–66
Population: early Christianity and urban, 31; immigration of rural (17th cen.), 64–65
Portugal, 86
Poverty in U.S., 115
Power: associational system and decentralization of, 116; defined, 17; ethnic and regional differences and, 57; fear of illegitimate, 117; in franchise, 102; of French and English aristocracies, 59–61; of government, 19, 78–79; influence compared with, 14; legislative, 19; monarchical, 65; money compared with, 27; separation of, in U.S., 91–94; 17th cen. system of, 54–56
Power élite, 116
Prestige: aristocratic, 59, 60, 83, 84; as communication node, 120–21; ethnic and regional differences and, 57; stratification system and, 13, 14; territorial monarchy and, 58
Priesthood: celibacy and hereditary consolidation of, 40; legitimation of, 40, 48
Privilege: educational revolution and, 96–97; economic, 116; French Revolution and legitimated, 79–81; rejected, 96, 97
Procedural institutions, 24–25
Production: development of mass, 107; differentiation through market economy and, 87; in U.S., 91–92; industrial revolution and, 76–78; money and level of, 27; social organization of process of, 22–23

Productive chain: extension of, 76
Professionalism: among artists, 108; associational development of, 26; collegial pattern of association and, 105–6; European, 131; new phase of, 98; Soviet, 127–28
Proletariat: bourgeoisie vs., 78, 115 (see also Bourgeoisie; Two-class system; Working class)
Property: market development and, 18, 22, 62, 63, 75, 79
Proprietorship: corporate control and, 104, 106; decline in agricultural, 110; occupational roles and, 108; U.S., landed, 90
Protestant Ethic, 69, 70
Protestant state churches, 49, 51, 54–55, 72
Protestantism: American, 49, 87–92; rights and religious toleration in, 21; conflict and, 141–42; distribution of, 50, 51; "God is dead" movement in, 99–100; religious pluralism and, 21, 49–57, 67, 72, 86, 88–91, 93, 98–99; secular culture and, 52
Protosocieties: collective organizations as, 2
Prussia, 1, 52, 53, 135; adaptive function emphasized by, 123; aristocracy of, 72–74, 132; civil service in, 104; collective organization of, 72–74; role of, in Europe, 72; weighted voting in, 82
Puritanism, 68, 69; in U.S., 87–88, 93

Radicalism, 117–19
Raphael, 46
Reality: systems of, 5
Reality sui generis: social systems as, 7, 8
Reformation, 46–49, 56, 67, 99, 129: Counter-Reformation and, 51–52, 71, 80, 129, 140; fraternity as embodiment of, 83; main developmental trend after, 67, 74; salvation and, 47–48, 54, 69–70
Relative deprivation, 109, 115, 116
Religion: constitutional rights and, 18; contemporary skepticism about, 99–100; cuius regio, eius religio formula and, 51, 54–56, 58, 88, 128; cultural innovation for, 29, 46, 47; as cultural system, 15; egalitarianism undermining, 119; legitimation of secular society by, 52–56; nationality and, 22; pluralism and, 21, 49–57, 67, 72, 86, 88–91, 93, 98–99; societal community and, 54–56; stratification of, 48, 49; value generalization and, 28; value legitimation through, 2, 9, 98–99; (see also Anticlerical-

Religion (Cont.):
ism; Christian Church; Christianity; Counter-Reformation; Protestantism; Roman Catholic Church; Roman Catholicism; Salvation)
Renaissance, 45–49, 99
Representative institutions: constituencies and, 102; development of, 61–63, 67, 87; political equality in, 82; (see also Democratic revolution; Electoral process; Franchise; Parliamentary system)
Resources: management of, 17; physical, for societal self-sufficiency, 8, 10
Revolution, 71–85; conflict and total, 142; differentiation in age of, 71–74; morality legitimating, 19 (see also Democratic, Educational, and Industrial Revolutions)
Revolutionaries, 118
Revolutionary act: collective goal-attainment and, 20
Rights: development of, 21–22, 62, 63, 67; egalitarianism and, 119; in French Revolution, 80–84; of government and citizen in Soviet Union, 126; in integrative societies of modern system, 132; welfare as, 21–22, 83, 93, 110, 132
Role-pluralism: defined, 12; stratification and, 13–14
Roles: bureaucratic organization and occupational, 23; defined, 6–8
Roman Catholic Church: boundaries of, 41; Counter-Reformation, 51–52, 71, 80, 129, 140; French Right and, 84; political and economic involvement of, 41; Renaissance arts and, 45; as social system, 10
Roman Catholicism: common language and U.S., 90; conflict and, 141; distribution of, 50, 51; ecumenism and, 99; English repression of, 55, 56; ethnicity and, 57; Germany and, 73, 74; religion pluralism and, 72, 88; secular culture and, 52; support for, 67
Roman Empire: early Church and, 31–33; institutional heritage of, 30, 34–36
Roman law, 35, 62, 64, 140
Roosevelt, Franklin D., 116
Rostow, Walt, 126
Rousseau, Jean-Jacques, 80
Russia: 41, 72, 85, 136; church of, 124–25; Communist Party, 125–27 (see also Soviet Union)
Russian Revolution, 124–29, 142

Salvation, 31; mediated by sacraments, 34, 47–48, 94; unmediated, 47–48, 54, 69–70
Salvinism, 72

151

index

Sartre, Jean-Paul, 99–100
Scandinavia, 53, 131–32
Scholastic philosophy, 45–47
Sciences, 46, 69, 70, 96, 99, 127 (see also Social sciences)
Secondary education: extension of, 95
Secular culture: of Church, 38–40; development of, 86–88; differentiation of, from society, 52
Secular society: alienation from, 31–34
Secularization: educational revolution and, 101; religious pluralism as process of, 98, 99
Self-interest in individualistic social theory, 12–13
Self-sufficiency: societal, 8–10
Smith, Adam, 62, 77, 80
Social sciences, 95, 96; continuity of society, culture and, 2; ideology and, 138
Social security, 130, 132 (see also Welfare)
Social systems: as constituents of action systems, 4–8; cultural systems compared with, 10
Social thinkers: first, 47
Socialism, 2, 117, 132; equal opportunity and, 114; vs. capitalism, 78, 96–97, 106–8, 111, 121; "in one country," 128; U.S. labor unions and, 109
Societal community: associational organization in, 24–26; citizenship as basis for inclusion in U.S., 92–93; crisis in, 118–21, 143; defined, 13, 56; differentiation in, 12–17; economy and, 17–18; as integrative subsystem, 11; market systems, bureaucratic organization and, 22–24; pattern maintenance and (defined) 14–15, (modern) 98–101; religion and 17th cen., 54–56; structure of modern, 43, 87–94; U.S. as new type of, 114–23; (see also Polity and,)
Society: defined, 8–10; (see also Subsystems of society)
Soviet Union, 97, 124–29, 132, 135; economy of, 123–26; ideology of, 124; working class in, 133
Spain, 41, 86, 107; as frozen society, 71–72; isolation of, 131; religious struggle and, 50, 52
Stalin, Joseph, 126, 127
Standards of living: upgrading, 112–14
State, the: authoritarian, 84; emergence of modern, 58, 67, 84; Prussian, 73
Steam engine, 77
Stratification system: ascriptive vs. nonascriptive, 96–97; described, 13–14; educational system and, 101; egalitarianism undermining, 119; family, 96; of integrative so-

Stratification system (Cont.):
cieties, 130–33; of religion, 48, 49; U.S. patterns of, 90–93, 119–21, 133; (see also Classes)
Student unrest: basis of, 117–18, 133–34
Subsystems of action: functional distinctions among, 4–5; interrelations among, 5–7
Subsystems of society, 10–25; defined, 10–12; methods of integration and, 18–26; (see also Societal community)
Suffrage: universal, 82, 101 (see also Franchise)
Superego, 6
Sweden, 132
Switzerland, 50, 51, 53, 131

Technological unemployment, 109–10
Technology: applied science and, 96; in industrial revolution, 75, 77; Soviet, 127
Territorial states: basis for division into, 57; emergence of, 42–43, 52–54, 58
Territoriality: early Church and, 30, 31; kingship principle and, 38, 58, 79; law and, 35, 36; membership in societal community and, 20; nationality and, 22; Protestant fragmentation and, 51; for societal self-sufficiency, 8–10
Theology, 45–48: early Christian, 31–32; Reformation, 47; Renaissance and, 45; scholastic, 45–48
Thirty Years War, 51
Thomism, 45–48
Tocqueville, Alexis de, 87, 123
Town and country: medieval differentiation between, 66
Transportation: industrial revolution and, 75–77
Trinity: theological ordering of, 31–32
Troeltsch, 32, 35
Two-class system: of early capitalism, 78; fraternity and, 83–84; (see also Bourgeoisie; Working class)

Ultimate reality: action systems and, 5; pattern-maintenance subsystem and, 10
United Nations, 131
United States: 85–121, 129, 132, 140; agriculture of, 110, 136; associational pattern of social development of, 96; citizenship in, 92–94; civil service in, 104; development of occupational roles in, 87, 108–12; differentiation of societal community and religious system in, 56; economy of, 106–14; educational revolution in, 127, 133; political system of, 82–83; financial markets in, 76; as first new nation, 87;

United States (Cont.):
ideology of, 124; legal system of, 18, 91, 93, 108; new type of societal community in, 114–23; pattern-maintenance system in, 98–101; Protestantism in, 49, 87–92; religious pluralism in, 87–91, 98–99; stratification system of, 90–93, 119–21, 133
Universities, 95, 98; equalization of membership in, 104; Soviet, 127–28; student unrest in, 117–18, 133–34
Urban communities: aristocracy of, 39, 41–42; development of, 41–44; Renaissance and, 47; secular Christian structures and, 38–40
Urbanization of industrial society, 77
Usury, 76

Value generalization: defined, 11, 15, 26, 27; intellectual alienation in, 100; in U.S., 98–99
Value systems: category of commitments in, 14–15; defined, 6–8; equality and commitments in, 120–21; institutionalization of modern, 137; legitimation of, 2, 9–10, 13, 14, 98–99; stability in patterns of, 92, 118, 123–24; (see also Pattern maintenance)
Vassalage, 37
Vietnam war, 128
Voluntary association: church as, 88; defined, 24; early Church as, 31, 32; U.S. as, 92–93
Voting: decision by, 25; as power, 17; secrecy of ballot and, 83; weighting votes, 82; (see also Electoral process)

War, 128, 141
Wealth: ethnic and regional differences and, 57
Weber, Max: bureaucratization and, 87, 103; influence of, 1–3; legitimate order and, 11; moral element in labor and, 17; process of rationalization and, 143; problem of meaning and, 5; Protestant Ethic and, 69, 70; view of Western social development, 38, 139
Welfare: as right, 21–22, 83, 93, 110, 132
Western Christianity: cultural system of, 10
Westphalia, Treaty of, 51
William the Conqueror, 44
Women, 101, 108, 114
Working class: class consciousness of U.S., 91; emergence of English, 64–65; French, 129; in integrative societies, 133; as leisure class, 112; U.S., 107–11; (see also Labor force; Labor unions)

152

index